The Process of Kafka's *Trial*

THE
PROCESS
OF
KAFKA'S
TRIAL

———

by

Adrian Jaffe

MICHIGAN

STATE

UNIVERSITY

PRESS

1967

Copyright © 1967
Michigan State University Press
Library of Congress Catalog Card Number: 67-24787

Manufactured in the United States of America

For Nancy

CONTENTS

vii

Contents

PREFACE

I have a number of debts, public and private, for which I hope this book can be tentative tender.

Among the private ones are those to Professor Rosalie L. Colie, Professor Lyle Blair, Professor Lore Metzger, Mrs. Jean Busfield, and my wife.

The public ones are to the staff of Olin Library, Washington University, who gave me generous and important help; and to the Departments of English at Michigan State University and Washington University, who provided time, space, and opportunity.

INTRODUCTION

Even if it would not be an act of critical *hubris*,[1] in the face
of all the writing which has been devoted to Kafka and to
The Trial, to promulgate another interpretation, this has not
in any case been my purpose. There is dearth neither of general
criticism of Kafka nor of particular points of view, and
almost anybody can find something to his taste. Among the
most venerable critical attitudes are those of theology[2] and
spiritual history,[3] with appropriate sectarian subdivisions into
Jewish[4] and Catholic.[5] Of more recent interest are interpretations of Kafka's work from the points of view of sociology,[6]
economics,[7] and psychology.[8] To say that psychological critics

[1] Professor Rosalie L. Colie would have here added "if not of
chutzpah." *Vide* her *Paradoxia Epidemica*, Princeton: Princeton University Press, 1966, p. 30, n. 43.

[2] Max Brod is the most important of the theological critics, not
necessarily because of any special acuity but because it has been assumed
that his friendship with Kafka must have given him a peculiar insight.
Another reason is the gratitude which is felt towards him for not having
destroyed the bulk of Kafka's manuscripts. Without Brod, the occupation of the Kafka critic, like that of Othello, would be gone. *Vide* in
particular Brod's *Franz Kafka: eine biographie*, Prague: Heinrich Mercy
sohn, 1937.

[3] *Vide*, as an excellent example, Robert Rochefort, *Kafka ou l'irréducible espoir*, Paris: R. Julliard, 1947.

[4] *Echt* examples are André Nemeth, *Kafka ou le mystère juif*, trans.
Victor Hintz. Paris: J. Vigneau, 1947; and Martin Buber, *Two Types
of Faith*, New York and London: Macmillan Company, 1951.

[5] Such as the article by John Kelly, "Franz Kafka's *Trial* and the
Theology of Crisis," *Southern Review*, V, Spring (1940), 748–766; and
portions of the book by Carryl Houselander, *Guilt*, New York: Sheed &
Ward, 1951.

[6] *Vide* Rudolf Fuchs, "Social Awareness," *The Kafka Problem*, ed.
Angel Flores. Norfolk, Conn.: New Directions, 1946, pp. 247–250.

[7] Edwin Berry Burgum, "Kafka and the Bankruptcy of Faith,"
Accent, III, Spring (1943), 153–167.

[8] *Vide* Charles Nieder, *The Frozen Sea*, New York: Oxford Univer-

Introduction

have had a field day with Kafka is to put it very mildly indeed. He is, after all, much more interesting than many of the patients who come to the offices of psychiatrists seeking help. We learn from Paul Goodman, for example, that the knife which ends Joseph K.'s life is "surely the satisfying penis that will transmute the persecution into love," and that it is "also a weapon of castration."[9] The novel is in effect a study of "the loss of erective potency in anxiety."[10] Charles Nieder points out that in the first chapter of *The Trial*, "The pleats, pockets, buttons and belt of the first warder are all sexual symbols. Others are nightshirt, underwear, thirtieth birthday (use of trinity), dipping bread-and-butter [sic] into honey pot, pincushion. . . ."[11] On a simpler and more general level, Hermann Uyttersprot finds *The Trial* to be a symbolic depiction of neurasthenia and hypochondria.[12] These are but a few, *cum multis aliis*, of what H. S. Reiss most appositely calls the "terribles simplificateurs."[13] I do not separate myself from their company from any lack of respect. To paraphrase some lines from Tennyson's *Ulysses*, they are decent not to fail in paying meet adoration to their household gods. They work their work, "I mine."

I conceive my work as that of trying to open up the text, to

---

sity Press, 1948; and Paul Goodman, *Kafka's Prayer*, New York: Vanguard Press, 1947.

[9] Goodman, *op. cit.*, p. 169.

[10] *Ibid.*, p. 161. Goodman, however, offers an escape to those who do not wish to read *The Trial* in this fashion. He says that "Franz Kafka was not a master theologian, yet a very remarkable one," whose "theology is original." (pp. 52–53) As a matter of fact, "Kafka is a far superior theologian to Kierkegaard." (p. 36) It is somewhat difficult to reconcile these two statements, or either of them with the dominant Freudian theme of the book.

[11] Nieder, *op. cit.*, p. 154.

[12] "Zur Struktur von Kafkas 'Der Prozess.' Versuch einer Neuordnung," *Langues Vivantes*, XIX (1953), 333–376.

[13] "Recent Kafka Criticism (1944–1955)—A Survey," *German Life and Letters*, ed. James Boyd, Leonard Forster, and C. P. Magill. Oxford: Basil Blackwell & Mott, 1953.

Introduction

unfold it, in a manner of speaking, and to arrive in this fashion at an understanding not only of the text itself but of the areas outside the text to which it leads by analogue. I should consider conclusions about the nature of Franz Kafka himself not to be within the venue of this study. And I know of no other way of opening up a text than to address my attention to it, and to it alone.

It is obvious that a study of a text will lead to some insights into the character of him who produced it, but it seems to me that such insights, and such conclusions as may be drawn from them, are essentially tautological. It is clear that what an author writes is a production of the author, and a deliberate production at that. It is inconceivable, therefore, that there should be no relationship between the artist and the *objet d'art* which he creates; on the contrary, the relationship is an intimate one. *Ça saute*, I should imagine, *aux yeux*. It is another way of saying that a given work could only have been produced by the man who produced it, at the time and in the circumstances of its production, and I believe that works of art have this quality of uniqueness. I also believe that we know this, and I have some doubts about the desirability in criticism of either belaboring or demonstrating the obvious. Moreover, as Maryse Choisy points out, there is a certain insolence involved:

> Cela me rappelle l'étonnante légèreté avec laquelle beaucoup de psychanalystes approchent l'aventure de Kafka. 'S'il avait été psychanalysé, disent-ils, il n'aurait pas écrit *Le Château* ou *Le Procès*. Il aurait écrit autre chose.' C'est tout juste s'ils n'ajoutent pas avec cette insolence de ceux qui estiment que la psychanalyse leur accorde la science infuse et le droit de s'ériger en critique d'art: 'Il aurait écrit quelque chose de mieux.'[14]

It is a matter of direction and intent. I think that an examination of a work which is undertaken in order to gain informa-

[14] "Peut-on Psychanalyser un Artiste?" *Psyché*, No. 54 (April 1951), 202.

3

Introduction

tion about the author is irrelevant for two reasons: (a) the only reason there is any desire to learn about the author is that another kind of judgment, that his works are artistically important, has already been made from the works themselves; (b) it makes the error of assuming that the text was written in order to provide information, not, as I believe, as a reflection.

The recent incursion into the field of literary criticism by psychiatrists has interested me, in this connection, not only because I have been pleased to note that they apparently have enough free time in their practices to devote themselves to literature, but because their interest is invariably directed to the psychoanalysis of writers who have come to their attention in the first place because literary critics have said, from an examination of their works, that they are important writers. Joyce and Kafka and Shakespeare, consequently, have not lacked for competent medical attention: it is regrettable that it should have had to be made available to them posthumously. But I have seen no concern, on the part of the psychiatrists in criticism, with the neurotic problems of such authors as Cornelius Mathews or James Lane Allen, precisely, I suspect, because the one is the author of *The Career of Puffer Hopkins* and the other of *The Bride of the Mistletoe*, rather than of *Ulysses, The Trial* or *Othello*. It would be unfortunate if, in their offices, psychiatrists refused their services to patients who were not interesting, or creative.

Apart from this, however, the psychiatrist *uses* literature as evidence for conclusions within his own field, which stands apart from literature in the first place. He is not alone in this: sociologists and theologians do the same thing. I think of this sort of activity as converting art into grist. The process seems to be that there are a number of statements about the nature of man (theological, societal, psychological) which have been made on the basis of careful study of man, and which can in many cases be demonstrated to have validity. I have no reason

4

to doubt that the field of psychiatry offers a valid and demonstrable interpretation of the condition of man, nor that statements from other disciplines, such as anthropology and sociology, do so as well. If they are true, they are not true because the professional scholars say so; they are true of man, and the scholars have codified and demonstrated this truth, not invented it. If they are true of man, or of any of his activities, they will of course be reflected in the activities of man, and perhaps most importantly in his most important activity, the creation of art.[15]

For this reason, it seems to me that all of these things, even if they had not been made the subject of separate study, are capable of being extrapolated from the work of art, not necessarily in the form of scientific demonstration, but in their essential quality. If it had not been discovered objectively that words are often symbolic of concealed and confused motives, for example, the fact that they are would have been indicated from a reading of Phaedra's speeches concerning the course of her feelings towards Hippolytus. I have a feeling that this kind of criticism approaches the problem from the wrong end—it goes into the work with the body of knowledge about the human condition derived from observation of life and then says, in effect, "aha, here is another piece of evidence that what I know about life is true." The trouble is that it is then assumed that this was the purpose of the text, and hence its "meaning," and its "significance." The text becomes an example of something already known, and a confirmation, rather than the container of all the aspects of life which come from its being "plugged in," so to speak, to life, and reflective of it. Which is not to say that exterior knowledge does not serve to extend

[15] "Avec le réel du psychiatre le poète est toujours un schizoïde. . . . Croire à l'âme d'une machine plutôt que tourner habilement ses manettes est grave pour un ingénieur, mais indispensable au poète." Maryse Choisy, *op. cit.*, p. 196.

5

the limits of awareness of the implications and analogous configurations within a text.[16] Certainly, as Frederic Will points
out, such studies as Ernest Jones' *Hamlet and Oedipus*,[17] and
Maud Bodkin's *Archetypal Patterns in Poetry*[18] suggest "unexpected perspectives," but I find it hard to agree with Will
that a knowledge of when he began toilet training "would
probably help us to understand Sophocles' literary achievement."[19]

I cannot resist indicating another difficulty which arises when
the critical direction is from the outside in, rather than the
other way about, and this has to do with the problem of intent.
Since a work of literature is contrived, it contains nothing
within it which does not serve the writer's intention, whatever

[16] For example, Mark Spilka (*Dickens and Kafka*, Bloomington:
Indiana University Press, 1963, p. 257) makes the point that Joseph K.
"is the victim, essentially, of sexual arrest—an abnormal prolongation of
the state of adolescence which is sometimes characterized by exorbitant
sexual fears and longings." Spilka, it appears, assumes that this is what
The Trial is all about, and that the Court is the tribunal which deals
with that sort of problem, or case. In short, Joseph K. *represents*
sexual arrest. I should like to suggest that while Joseph K. does not
represent sexual arrest and while the novel is not designed to say something about it, the *pattern* of sexual arrest and its consequent assaults
upon authority is certainly within the book, so that the book can lead
to a consideration of the psychological problem in the external world and
perhaps even to a deeper understanding of it. There are other analogous
configurations as well: it is better, I think, and less likely to produce
rigid imperatives, to think of the novel as an abstraction of relationships
rather than as the depiction of a given one. It is curious that Spilka,
who has impeached such critics as Edwin Honig, George Ford, Frederick
Hoffman and Edgar Johnson for being unable to resist the attempt to
use fixed categories of allegory in their analyses of Kafka (p. 96) should
not realize that he is doing the same thing, substituting Freudian psychology for the more traditional frameworks. I am indebted in this
connection to Professor Hazard Adams, who in the course of some con-
versations made the acute observation that psychology has become the
new allegorical referent.

[17] London: Oxford University Press, H. Milford, 1951.

[18] New York: Norton, 1949.

[19] *Literature Inside Out*, Cleveland: The Press of Western Reserve
University, 1966, p. 52.

that may be, and however conscious of its origins he may be. A literary structure is not a natural structure, like that of a snowflake whose symmetry is unintentional. Whatever relationships its parts bear to one another they bear because they have been deliberately placed in that particular juxtaposition. This quality is not diminished by any limitations which may have restricted the absolute choices available to the artist. Thus, responses in literature are not only responses *per se*, they are responses to stimuli which have been inserted, so to speak, *in order to* elicit them. It is precisely this which is not true of life. The situation which produces a neurotic response in a man, on the basis of which a trained analyst may be able to identify his condition, was not designed to produce this response. The patient in the psychiatrist's office says different things every time he comes for consultation, whereas Hamlet always says exactly the same thing. It is seriously open to question, in my mind, whether psychoanalysis, theology, sociology, anthropology and other disciplines can in fact be applied validly to men, or to experiences, which are to be found embedded in literary structures. I think they are exempt from this, and that it is this exemption which gives to art its uniqueness. On the other hand, these disciplines, which serve to widen our knowledge of the real world, can widen our appreciation of the analogous reflections of that real world which reside in art if only because art is quintessential. If we move out from the work, the world into which it may lead us is the more comprehensible for all the studies that have been made of its nature; if we move into the work, the work is less so.

A method seems to have emerged from, and to have been implied by, this discussion of the text of *The Trial*. My purpose was only to offer a reading, not to demonstrate a method. The fact that a method should have emerged seems to me to be evidence of the derivative implication of what I have tried to say, that there is an inviolable relationship between structure and content when we are dealing with an artistic creation, and

7

that structure is a bridge between two discourses of reality which connects and fuses them into an integral unity. Raymond Tschumi,[20] in setting out what he calls a "philosophy of literature," advances a number of points which my own study implies. I wish I had come upon Tschumi's work before I had written my own, but I find it interesting that to whatever extent I may have suggested some of the relationships which he outlines, I know that they came from inside the text and hence demonstrate, in the way in which I think of the term, their own validity. I want in addition to acknowledge a special and heavy debt to Günther Anders, upon whose acuity I have drawn, especially in Sections 8, 9, 12, and 13.

The method suggests the uniqueness of given structures to convey given states and the fact that the choice of these structures is inevitable. It suggests further that the writer cannot falsify the experience of his text by making an arbitrary selection of an inappropriate structure. It is a question of spatial relationships, of where one part of the structure stands with respect to another, and it is from these spatial relationships that we can derive the nature of the state. Victim, for example, is always receiver, object of a transitive action. It is this relationship to the action which constitutes his being victim, and so long as he remains in it, he will remain victim. Thus he also occupies a *situation* which embodies his not having responsibility for the results of the action, and his lack of responsibility is a function of his position, rather than a metaphysical concept. If he kills himself, for example, he converts himself into both doer and receiver and thus suicide, *per se*, is a structure for responsibility; if he is killed by somebody else, the responsibility lies elsewhere in the nature of the context. Thus a character must, if he is to "change" as a result of some evaluation of moral experience, be placed into another frame of the structure as well as "think" a new series of thoughts. In the same way, the process of symbolically recapitulating experi-

[20] *A Philosophy of Literature*, Philadelphia: Dufour Editions, 1962.

8

ence requires a movement *backwards* with respect to the point at which the process begins: backward movement, the state of moving away from another point, contains recapitulation. Henry Fleming, for example, in Crane's *The Red Badge of Courage*, flees from the front lines back to the rear echelons. His movement is inevitable and gives to his flight, in itself and apart from the particular symbols which Crane uses, its own recapitulative integrity. Again, when a character's value system is irrelevant, he is *outside* the world; if he were in it, the values would be relevant. The relevancy of the system is integral with the position of the man with respect to the world, not a separate, independent episteme. This position may be represented in various ways: Othello's blackness, Don Quixote's cavalier garb, but these are only ways, not essential elements. Since Othello is outside, and Desdemona is inside, it is indeed offensive to sense that she should have run to the sooty bosom of such as he. The structure of their relationship makes its failure inevitable quite apart from such effect upon it as Iago may have had. Being outside, Othello cannot enter, but can only try to change his position by destroying the inside—hence there is no structural possibility that he should not kill his wife.

Relationships, then, have consequences, and since the relationships are in a structure, they are not within the arbitrary decision of the writer. Furthermore, as it is a reciprocal matter, the consequence can be derived from the structure which contains it, and can be properly viewed as the consequence of condition and hence as its nature, face to face. It converts the *representativeness* of a literary character to *unique condition*, strips away the allusive element in metaphor and insists that the starting point is the articulation of the bones of the text. It suggests that a work of literature is an interior counterpart of non-literary experience and its reflected image, not the other way around. It suggests a dimension of artistic necessity which is neither aesthetic nor philosophical. It suggests something else as well, and I think this deserves mention because there lurks

9

over contextual criticism a certain soft impeachment. Ronald Gray puts it well:

> In discussing *The Trial*, it began to emerge a little, I thought, that the disastrous beliefs in which the novel was conceived had also been disastrous for its literary form . . . It may be . . . that the pursuit of a fuller appreciation of purely literary matters will end by coinciding with a fuller appreciation in other spheres.[21]

And finally it suggests the obligation to focus attention upon how things work, upon their function. For art does not exist in nature; it is always created, put together. It is an ordering of experience and it is more useful, I think, to concentrate upon the order than upon the experience. The experience is the order. The order is embedded in the structure. Art therefore has a total impact and an inevitable one, which "means" only itself.[22] I think that *The Trial*, which is functionally and structurally a reversal of the ordinary and the traditional, is the unique way in which this reversal can be conveyed. It doesn't stand for it, but is the reversal itself.

[21] Introduction to *Kafka*, Englewood Cliffs, N. J.: Prentice-Hall, Inc., 1962, p. 8.

[22] On re-reading the text of the unpublished paper, "What is an Approach?" which Professor E. D. Hirsch, Jr., offered at the 1966 Modern Literature Conference at Michigan State University, and to which he has graciously invited me to refer, I have a feeling that we are very close in arguing for the uniqueness of the literary work, but apart insofar as Professor Hirsch seems to be convinced that there is, beyond the meaning which he may find in a text, a transcendental "meaning" of an absolute order, the discovery of which is the critic's task. He thus rejects what he calls "naive perspectivism" and objects to the possibility that a reader may entertain only his own "perspective-ridden" meaning. This gloomily suggests that the reader's perspectives may be of a random kind, leading to Heaven knows what. I am inclined to think that the structural relationships control the range of these perspectives precisely in proportion as they have analogues in experiences external to the text. I should therefore view the problem of reading in two senses of Sartre's term "création dirigée," one which embodies Sartre's notion of the reciprocity of images, another in the sense that the direction is locked into the structure.

Introduction

Changes in our perception of the nature of the world will therefore be accompanied by changes in the *structure* of literature. It is not a matter of saying new things within older genres; rather, the genre and that which it is alone able to convey are indivisible. Since its modifications come not from aesthetic choice but from a recognition of unique appropriateness, these changes in perceptions may be adduced from an examination of the structures, which imply as well as contain them. Literary structures therefore have assumptions as their foundations, and art is the empire of assumptions. It does not really matter whether these assumptions have any scientific, empirical, or objective accuracy—they function anyway. The literary structure is thus the projection of the action "as if," from which we can derive the hypotheses. I note towards the end of my study the way in which actions "as if" provide energy. I refer in that context to the characters of *The Trial*, but it is also true of artists, for if art is the embodiment of "as if" it is also, as I think we all appreciate, for that reason the most energetic activity, the most vital *élan*, of all. It affirms life as nothing else does, and we should not be surprised that it is the only activity of man which has no death.

This has not, in one sense, been an easy book to write, since, as Professor Colie points out, academic discourse conventionally requires a developmental order. But since this is not how *The Trial* works; since, indeed, it assumes and embodies the absence of developmental order, I have found it more appropriate to allow the reader to be "at once naturalized and surprised by the passage from one subject to the 'next,' "[23] as he is when he reads the novel. To have succumbed to a rage for order would, I think, have falsified my objectives. For I am primarily concerned with the process. I do not want to impose a chronology upon an experience which has neither beginning nor end. Hermann Uyttersprot is thus right and wrong when he argues for a rearrangement of the chapters

[23] *Paradoxia Epidemica*, pp. 38–39.

11

according to internal chronology.[24] He is right because his arrangement would be more closely related to a temporal sequence; he is wrong because temporal sequence is of no importance in a novel in which time has been suspended.

The Trial is not the less for not having been put together as Uyttersprot suggests, nor would it be the more if it had been. It is of no consequence at all that my discussion of *The Trial*, although it starts with the first line, should move through, rather than along, the sequence of episodes. If it had been possible, I should have liked to call the book "Esquisse pour une lecture" of *The Trial*. English does not quite permit this, however.

I fully share Hugh Kenner's wish that there were illustrations to keep the reader from dwelling on the paucity of documentation.[25] All quotations from *The Trial* are from the translation of Edwin and Willa Muir, which is available in so many different editions that page references would have been pointless. I used the Penguin edition of 1953.

St. Louis, Missouri   A. J.
November, 1966

[24] *Op. cit.* Also "Zur Struktur von Kafkas Romanen," *Langues Vivantes*, XX (1954), 367–383. Uyttersprot's suggested order of the chapters is as follows:

I: The Arrest (no change)	VI: K.'s Uncle (no change)
II: Fräulein Bürstner's Friend	VII: In the Cathedral
III: First Interrogation	VIII: Advocate
IV: In the Empty Interrogation Chambers	IX: The Commercial Traveller
V: The Whipper (no change)	X: The End

Uyttersprot argues for the same order in his *Eine Neue Ordnung der Werke Kafkas? Zur Struktur von 'Der Prozess' und 'Amerika,'* Antwerp: C. De Vries-Brouwers, 1957.

[25] Author's Note in *Flaubert, Joyce and Beckett, The Stoic Comedians*, London: W. H. Allen, 1964.

PART I

1.

The Function of Name

"Someone must have been telling lies about Joseph K., for without having done anything wrong he was arrested one fine morning." These opening words of Kafka's *The Trial* subsume a number of the critical problems of the text.

The question of whether or not the "K" stands for "Kafka" is less important than the fact that the protagonist has been deliberately deprived of a surname. (In *The Castle* the given name will be entirely dropped, of course.) Surnames have certain functions and have certain effects, in general and within the purely literary context. In general, they are class names which serve to indicate that an individual belongs to a larger class which is none the less distinguished from other classes. They suggest that he must have a minimum number of characteristics in common with the other members of his class which none of the members of the class, including himself, shares with other classes. Such an individual is thus given two contradictory aspects: he has a series of collateral relationships with other human beings in terms of which his particular nature may be perceived and implicitly, though partially, understood; and he is presented as not being a number of things which it would be perfectly plausible for him to be. The implication in literary analysis is that the behavior of the individual is to be seen in the first place as a function of his class membership, and is above all not to be seen as applicable, to the same extent, to persons not of this class. A surname, for example, which is clearly of a particular nationality, cannot avoid the suggestion that at the least the nationality is significant, and to the extent

13

that the nationality is significant, it may be presumed that a certain number of literary purposes would not have been so well served if the nationality had been different. It may be argued that there is a tendency on the part of a writer, in the absence of any particular requirement, to assign to his characters his own nationality, since, in thinking about people in general, his own nationality is more "normal." This is without doubt true, but it changes the principle only in degree. We may conclude that when the nationality of a character is the same as that of the author, the nationality has less significance analytically than when it is different, which is not to say that it has no significance at all. One significance which it will retain is certainly that if we assume that a writer chooses his own nationality only in the absence of any particular requirement, his choice of his own nationality will demonstrate that there was no particular requirement to choose another, and we can further assume that whatever national traits the character may have are either of only incidental importance, or are generally similar to those found elsewhere. When an author gives a nationality to a character which is different from his own, we are justified in asking what particular purposes he intended, by this choice, to serve—we cannot dismiss this choice as having insignificant bearing on the text. In his short story *The Dry Rock*, for example, Irwin Shaw chooses to give a Russian name, Tarloff, to the taxi driver whose inability to make clear his notions of justice end by stranding him, so to speak, upon the dry rock of principle. We cannot avoid the assumption that this name has a function of a particular kind, since otherwise there would seem to have been no point in using other than an American surname. Such an assumption leads to some possible conclusions: that the irony of the story is carried largely by the circumstance that it is a foreigner who upholds the principles of America which Americans no longer care very much about; and that the impact of the irony is increased by the circumstance that the Czarist society which the Russian came to America to escape represents not only an especially odious kind of tyranny, but is the diametric opposite of the symbolic American experience. In cases where the function of nationality is not clear, it is certainly important that the critic continue to assume it and to look for it. *Flesh*, a novel by Brigid Brophy, is a case in point. The two major characters are Jewish. It is reasonable to assume that the Jewishness of the major characters is designed to function in some special way which could not be accomplished otherwise. When an initial reading of the text fails to disclose anything which would not have been perfectly plausible if the characters had not been Jewish, the possibility must be held open that somewhere the reader has failed to perceive something, not necessarily something which was the product of the author's conscious mind, but something none the less. In short, specific nationality, and its smaller classes set by the boundaries of surnames, can never be gratuitous.[1]

There thus flow from a character with a surname a number of consequences which have a bearing upon the way in which the reader will understand him and hence upon the ways in which the text is able to function. A named character is, to a greater or lesser extent, confined to the possibilities, theoretically finite, which are open to members of his class. When none of these limitations is in fact germane, and when, in addition, they would tend to falsify the experience, it is necessary to get rid of the surname and of all its complications, entirely. Hence "K.," the minimum necessary to designate a man.

The state of being a man is, of course, a condition, and since

---

[1] I cannot agree with the conclusion of Albert Camus that in *The Trial* "Le héros aurait pu s'appeler Schmidt ou Franz Kafka." (*Le Mythe de Sisyphe*, Paris: Gallimard, 1942, p. 175). On the contrary, I think the results would have been devastating.

all men are in such a condition, there is a tendency to think of the literary treatment of a character such as K. as yet another example of what has been called "Everyman." There are a number of reasons having to do with the nature of allegory, with which we shall be concerned presently, which suggest that in *The Trial* this is misleading, but there are other reasons as well. Conditions, including the human condition, may be partial or whole in the sense that variations are possible in the degree to which a given man shares all of the human possibilities, and in the extent to which he responds to any of the series of potential stimuli open to his state of being. While he cannot escape the fundamental confinement within the condition, this only means that in the nature of things he can never operate outside of it. It does not mean that within it he must operate in any particular way. The universality of experience which is a prerequisite to the notion of "Everyman" diminishes as the characteristics of the protagonist become more particular. Failure to remain aware of this can lead to certain misconceptions in our understanding of tragedy, for example, where we think we see the fall of man but really see the fall of particular men who belong to the general class but occupy within it a smaller one. Oedipus has an arrogance which is human but which is not the necessary property of either any man or of any king. The ambiguity in the play arises in part from the fact that he cannot fall as victim of his condition without also falling as vehicle of his arrogance. The first could never have been avoided (which constitutes the nature of the murky irony of Jocasta's point of view) but the second, not being inherently concomitant, could well have been.

The circumstance, therefore, that K. is presented with no further name can logically suggest that he is "Everyman" only to the extent that he fails to have significantly particular characteristics (apart from those which would in any case have been implied by a full name). In fact K. has a number of particular characteristics which emerge in the course of the novel, to the presence of which it is reasonable to attribute a salient proportion of the course of his career: he is certainly a social snob, he has a great deal of self-importance, he is — intellectually arrogant, and, above all, he is seemingly incapable of loving and, hence, of being loved. In view of this it is doubtful if the interpretation of the single initial as "Everyman" is — useful, and such an interpretation may lead to the mistake, in reading Kafka, of looking "at what he is driving at rather than at what he says."[2]

2.

Process and the Figure of the Law

"Someone must have been telling lies about Joseph K., for without having done anything wrong he was arrested one fine morning." The word "for" opens up a number of important aspects, not only of these lines but, in a compressed fashion, of the novel as a whole. The inherent presupposition, almost always shared in the initial instance by the reader, is that the act in question, the arrest, is and must be the conclusion of a set of anterior acts, linked together in some sort of orderly process. We can characterize this presupposition by saying that it first of all rejects the possibility that it is an act in isolation; second, that it is seen as an end result, a terminal effect, of anterior causes; third, that these causes are not themselves isolated but are parts of a chain of causes and effects related to the presence of a system.

Now if we are confronted with an act which is in fact the

[2] Ronald Gray, *Kafka's Castle*, Cambridge University Press, 1956, p. 1.

final effect of an anterior chain of causes and effects, we assume the anterior chain from the act itself. If, in addition, these causes are systematic, the act causes us to recognize that we have become involved in a system; and if we proceed to believe that we should not be, we have no reason to question the system, only its applicability to us. We do this by seeking flaws in the assumed chain.

To begin with, we may restrict our consideration to the system suggested by Kafka in these opening lines, that of the law. An arrest presupposes an officer who makes the arrest. Officers are distinguished from other classes of men by the circumstance that at a certain point, but always anterior to their functioning in an official capacity, they have been designated as officers by an authority competent to make such designations. These designations may, if necessary, be proved by some sort of paper, but are often taken for granted when the officer wears some mark of his position, such as a uniform or a badge of some sort. All officers, however, are not empowered to make arrests—to move from the general class of officer to the particular class of arresting officer, there must be a further specific designation, often a warrant. For a warrant to be effective, it must have been issued by an authority competent to do so, a member of that sub-class of legal officials who are justices. The conditions, however, under which justices may issue warrants are specific. They may do so only when somebody appears before them to make a complaint. The kind of complaint which may result in the issuance of a warrant is in turn not general but specific. It must allege, and allege to the satisfaction of the justice, at least two things: (1) that a certain act was committed and (2) that this act was prohibited by a statute. The statute may not be any list of acts which are to be prohibited, but only those embodied in laws which have been passed by bodies competent to pass them. The nature of this competence resides in turn in other laws, often constitutional, which regulate the circumstances, such as election, under which competent legislative bodies may come into existence.

The idiosyncratic features of such a legal system are not important—the laws can be issued by fiat, the justice can be a clerk, the statutes can be general, they can relate to moral standards or to secular, some of the steps may be omitted, or shortened—but there remains a system, so that it is reasonable and accurate to assume that an arrest has occurred as the result of a certain series of necessary preconditions.

The judgment of the wrongness of such an arrest, consequently, must be in terms of the systematic chain of which it is the final product, and it can be of two kinds: (1) there has been a flaw in the process itself and (2) although there has been no flaw, it is not justified in terms of some other standard of conduct. In the system suggested, it is instructive to examine several possible flaws: (1) the arresting officer is either not an officer at all or is not an officer authorized to make an arrest; (2) the officer is not authorized to make an arrest either because he has no warrant or because the warrant which he has was not issued by an authority competent to issue warrants; (3) the authority who issued the warrant was not competent to do so either because he was not a designated justice or because the complaint upon which he acted was not in the class of competent complaints; (4) the complaint was not competent because it alleged an act which was not prohibited by statute or an act which was prohibited by a statute which had no force; (5) the statute had no force because it was in contradiction to other controlling laws, such as constitutional provisions, or because it was not passed properly; (6) the statute was not passed properly because the body which passed it was not properly constituted or because it was not passed in accordance with the process governing the passage of such laws, including, for example, approval of a governor or a recorded voting majority in its favor.

The nature of "justice," therefore, is very often a function of the validity of process. "Injustice" may be said to have taken place where a process has continued despite an anterior flaw which ideally should have prevented it from going farther, so that rectification can be made if a way can be found of returning the issue to its point of last validity. Flaws can occur for a variety of reasons: mechanical, in which oversight or error have occurred; malicious, in which a step has been deliberately perverted for exterior motives; corrupt, in which a consideration has been offered to accomplish a desired deviation. If, upon arrest, we assume, as does K., that we have "done nothing wrong"—that no action of ours, as far as we can determine, has fallen within the category of prohibited actions from which all subsequent legal process must necessarily stem—we can only conclude that we are the victims of anterior flaw, and choosing to ignore for the moment the other considerations which are possible, K. comes to the immediate conclusion that while the process has been inherently orderly, it was set into motion by a false allegation, since it is certain that there must have been an allegation and it is his opinion that in view of his own review of his conduct no allegation could possibly have been true. Thus "someone must have been telling lies . . ."

Characteristic of systems of this kind is the fact that they do not serve to clarify or to examine the bases upon which they are constructed. Their terms are curiously immanent, for they are not necessarily related (although in practice there may be a contingent relationship to another hierarchy of moral values) to any system of values outside of themselves. Law, in other words, has the force of law, and the only relevant issue is whether or not a certain act has been committed under circumstances which have been declared to be prohibited, not whether or not such an act should have been declared to be prohibited. Indeed, if we consider a moral system to constitute a form of abstract truth, at least to those who adhere to it, we can recognize that in what is called "judicial cognizance" nothing is relevant which has not come before the court competently, regardless of what may in fact have occurred. To illustrate, there are certain areas in which a wife is incompetent to testify against her husband. Any presumptions about the husband which can only be rebutted by the wife's testimony must always stand in the absence of competent testimony from another, whether or not these presumptions have any basis in so-called "fact."[3]

The law consequently embodies an implied truth, that things are right as they are presently constituted by the law, which in effect is the definition of truth, or rightness, as the *status quo*. The function of the law is often, as a result, that of providing a means of restoring any imbalance which may have occurred by virtue of actions which, since they are illegal actions, are presumed to unbalance the existing order and are hence, within such a meaning of the term, wrong. There thus arises the concept of "trespass," which in its primary meaning suggests the existence of a territory the inaccessibility of which without consent is deemed to represent the right order of things, and which, in its derived meaning, can be treated as including the abstract notion of trespass upon the rights of others, which it is proper that they hold undisturbed. Trespass of the first kind can be punished; trespass of the second kind cannot be punished, but an attempt can be made to restore the imbalance by the computation and enforcement of a payment in money.[4] In short, everybody has a right to remain where he is, and if anything should happen to move him, the law will undertake

[3] In bastardy cases, for example, in which the illegitimate paternity of the infant was inferred from the fact that the wife had refused access to the husband for a substantial period of time, the presumption of the husband's access could not be rebutted by the testimony of the wife that in fact he had not had any.

[4] In certain American states, for example, civil actions involving liability for negligence are actions in "trespass on the case," although the concept of "assumpsit" is often used to cover these actions as well as those founded upon contract.

Processes are not arbitrary but relate to the assumptions of the institutions of which they are a part. When institutions come into being, they do so in answer to certain needs and to certain goals which the society demands, and their particular formal processes are those which seem best able to achieve these goals. We have suggested, with respect to the law, a certain number of assumptions, and each step in the legal processes reflects these assumptions. We may say that each provision reflects, at a minimum, the strong statement that the condition which would obtain if the provision were not there would be intolerable, and such statements go back to larger statements, having the effect of moral force, about the ideal nature of the world. As an example, the provision that no arrest shall be made without a warrant clearly reflects the statement that it is intolerable to live in a world of arbitrary arrests, and the provision that no warrant shall issue in the absence of a valid complaint implies a repugnance for a society in which the legal processes can be put into motion by caprice or by subjective judgment. There is thus an integrity in every process between its special form and the interpretation of the nature of the world out of which it grows. The latter may, in the most accurate way, be deduced from the former.

The nature of things is such, however, that forms tend to change less readily than interpretations of experience, and at certain junctures, such as our own time, they may persist long after the views of the world of which they are an implied expression have died. In part this is due to the normal human reluctance to change; in part it is due to the tendency we have to confuse the form with the substance, and to assume from the presence of the one that we have the other, or at least, that the other is as closely related as it once was. The point is particularly clear with respect to the church, which is perhaps why so many religious interpretations of *The Trial* have been made. In this regard it is probably fair to say that the church may be an analogue of the experience of the novel, but the experience of the novel is not for that reason an analogue of the church. A case in point is the use, in many churches, of dead languages which none of the faithful understands. Prayers were originally couched in the only language in which they could be couched, that which the persons praying habitually used. Under these circumstances the prayer had at least this characteristic, that the person saying it knew what he was saying and hence had some reason to believe that he was communicating to the object of the prayer, which thus directly answered to a need and was satisfactorily valid. The death of these languages was not accompanied by a recasting of the prayer, so that, the original language once thoroughly interred, the prayer lost that part of its value which was related to the understanding of its terms by the person praying. Communication with God, therefore, underwent a change from direct expression to formal expression in terms of a frozen formula: religious experience thus inhered in the use of form, and became confused with the use of form, so that it could be held to exist when the form was present, and held to be absent when the form was absent.[5]

The forms of structures do not change, then, as rapidly as the structures themselves, and although they ultimately must, there are points in the development of human society where the structure has changed almost entirely but where new forms designed to reflect this change have not as yet come into being.

[5] When, in final recognition of the demise of Latin as a current language all over the world, the Catholic Church authorized masses in the language of the country, many faithful were convinced that these masses were not religiously valid and that they were being deprived of the experience for which they had come to church. The same kind of objection was made to revised versions of the Bible designed to offer a translation into modern English; it has long been assumed that there is a relationship between holiness, and sanctity of thought, and the particular qualities of the English of the King James version.

The persistence of the old forms, unfortunately, is taken to indicate the parallel persistence of the old structures, but in practice any effort to work within the old structures by the use of the old forms founders because the old structure is no longer there, and any effort to work within the new structure by the use of the old forms founders on the utter irrelevancy which they have.

3 ·

Accusation and Crime

Even if we put aside for the moment the larger analogues, the assumption may be made that Joseph K. is confronted with an act, that of his arrest, which does not presuppose the anterior system which he assumes, but another system, different *not necessarily* in its formal structure, but different in the interpretation of experience which it reflects. For it does not invariably follow that a set of forms which is germane to one order of postulates is for that reason inappropriate to another—and since no value inheres in forms *per se*, any form can accomplish a number of diverse purposes, always provided that it is not of such a nature as to contradict them. Within the initial figure of the law, then, an insight into the possible problem is gained if we propose that it is a crime to be accused of a crime. Such a proposition is offensive only to those persons who insist that accusations must be false or true, and that they must consequently be followed by some sort of process which will determine their truth or falsehood. There is no reason why such a view of the world should be superior to any other, and it is no less reasonable, although to many it may be a good deal less comfortable, to hypothesize that it is a crime to be accused, in which case, obviously, the "truth" or "falsity" of the accusation is supremely irrelevant. It should be recalled at this point that there is an integrity between a process and the interpretation of the world out of which it grows, and to which it provides a system of procedural manipulative techniques. These interpretations are not, any more than the processes themselves, arbitrary to those who make them, although they may appear to be so to those who make others. What they represent in the final analysis is a set of statements about the "true" nature of the world, based upon experiences with this world. There is no concomitant conclusion that this nature of the world is desirable, nor that it should not be regretted, nor that another condition might not be preferable—such evaluation does not affect the situation itself in the slightest. The formal processes which develop as means to make it possible to live within any given postulation of a "true" universe need only the justification that they are effective. They rely for their effectiveness not upon their inherent contours, but upon the degree to which the world in fact is, or is assumed to be, of that order which the forms are peculiarly able to reflect and hence to manipulate. Now the experiences of the world, the nature of the interpretation men make of the impact upon them of these experiences, can and do change, and if in fact it is the nature of things that no accusation takes place without cause, it follows without question that it is a crime to be accused. If it is a crime to be accused, there can be no unjustified arrest, and it is certainly not true that "someone must have been telling lies." When experience demonstrates that it is reasonable to hold that it is a crime to be accused, it does not follow that the forms of the older system need be abandoned in their entirety. A systematic method for bringing criminals to account is still important even though the essence of their criminality may have changed, and a hearing is no more useless when the matter is one of assessing, for example, degree or extent of guilt than when it is concerned with determining whether or not that guilt exists.

While it is not necessary that the older forms should be abandoned, there is of course no reason why they should be maintained with any degree of care or assiduity. On the contrary, neglect would seem to follow from irrelevance and to imply it.[6] The condition of the Advocates' room is a case in point: "It was lit only by a small skylight, which was so high up that if you wanted to look out, you had to get some colleague to hoist you on his back, and even then the smoke from the chimney close by choked you and blackened your face." When the Advocates no longer have a viable function, there is no reason to devote any effort to the conditions of their work. All that is required, in this late vestigial stage, is that there should be a room, for the Advocates have not disappeared. For the same reasons, the particular uniform which traditional society places upon its arresting officers need not be a particular uniform at all, so long as in one way or another it represents a style of dress not common. Styles of dress become uncommon largely through the passage of time and concurrent changes of fashion. When there is no further "fashion" in that sense of the word, there is no further need for the dress to change, and it may hence continue to be worn long after it has lost its original relationship to its function and long after it has ceased in general to be worn. Hence, the warder who arrests K. is dressed in what appears to be a "tourist's outfit," furnished with "all sorts of pleats, pockets, buckles, and buttons," the purpose of which has been lost even though it

[6] It is not without significance in this regard that Departments of English, French, German or Classics are most often to be found housed in the oldest buildings on the campus, and that professors in those fields often have to work in conditions resembling those of the hedge-advocates. Physics, Mathematics and related disciplines, on the contrary, usually have the most modern quarters.

"in consequence looked eminently practical." K., in being led to ask "Who are you?" confesses to his inability to recognize the function of the dress, although it is of sufficient peculiarity to make him understand that it must have one. It is doubtful if he would have asked this question of an officer dressed in customary police garb, although such a question is in either instance of critical importance. The man, however, ignores the question "as though his appearance needed no explanation . . . ," as in fact it does not if it is considered that he would not have appeared if there had been no reason for him to do so, and is in any case unaware of the possibility that the question has been motivated more by his dress than by his actions.

The world in which it is a crime to be accused is not, incidentally, so remote as it may appear at first consideration. During the period when Senator McCarthy was making his attacks upon "communists" in the United States, a large proportion of the public were convinced that nobody would have been subpoenaed to appear before the Senator's committee had there not been in the first place a strong likelihood that he was a communist—in fact, the term "communist" came to be defined as referring to a person who had been accused by Senator McCarthy of being one. One of the immediate results was that it became important for those who did not wish to be "convicted" of the crime of being communists to avoid, not the condition of being one, but the accusation. Fear of accusation was as effective within this universe as fear of a guilty verdict presumably is in the traditional one. In addition, all efforts on the part of the accused to deny their guilt, or to attack the procedure on the ground that it did not permit the full play of the adversary system by which the traditional court arrives at a determination of truth, failed completely because they did not take into account the circumstance that the accused would not have been there at all if their guilt had not already been determined, since in effect what they had to answer for was the crime of having been brought there. While in its developmental stages Senator McCarthy's committee made efforts to exclude or to inhibit legal counsel, at a later point it was understood that since legal counsel was irrelevant, there was no need, other than that of general convenience, to muzzle it, and no need to change the form of traditional hearing which the new hearing had unthinkingly adopted, perhaps because it was closest at hand.

One obstacle remained from the outmoded system, however, that of the so-called constitutional protection against self-incrimination. The irrelevancy of the concept of "self-incrimination" in a situation where the fact of being accused is the crime did not fail to strike a large number of people interested in justice, but they were inhibited from doing away with this protection by the circumstance that the constitutional amendment had became frozen in the passage of time into a holy text which could not be disturbed without running the risk of bringing down divine reprisal. They got out of this difficulty by adopting the point of view, which was obvious enough to them anyway, that to invoke the amendment was a clear admission of guilt, punishable by its own condign punishment, such as loss of job, i.e., expungement from the universe. Thus denial of guilt becomes evidence of guilt, a fact of which the Examining Magistrate is well aware when he says to K. at the end of the first interrogation: "today you have flung away with your own hands all the advantages which an interrogation invariably confers on an accused man."

4 ·

Irrelevancy and Allegory

If the initial assumption of Joseph K., that "someone must have been telling lies," is false, not in the sense that therefore someone must have been telling the truth, but rather in the sense that the fact of the arrest only means that something must have been said, any action he takes, and any response he has, will be an exercise in futility. This futility is a direct consequence of irrelevancy, and embodies its own consequence of increasing fatigue. For it is difficult for K., either in *The Trial* or in *The Castle*, to entertain the possibility that the futility of his actions stems from their irrelevancy rather than from themselves, and the problem may in fact be projected into a larger realm of general rather than specific irrelevancy.

The irrelevancy of K.'s actions is perceived by the reader when it is not even suspected by K. himself, although even here there is a certain resistance—inherent in the normal processes of reading as well as in the normal, perhaps smug, assumptions of the existence of an orderly universe—which postpones this perception for a period of time and thus ascribes the feeling of discomfort to the confrontation with a nightmare.[7] This perception of irrelevancy as perhaps the major concern of *The Trial* is not essentially incorrect, but it can lead, and often has led, to a futile concern with its specific applicability, so that one or another allegorical interpretation comes to mind: that Kafka is treating the breakdown of meaningful process in

[7] In this connection it is interesting to note that a number of Kafka's stories, notably *In the Penal Colony* and *Metamorphosis,* have appeared in paperback collections of "horror stories" or "fantastic tales," guaranteed to chill the reader and to keep him glued to his chair.

bourgeois society through an examination of the failure of its legal and bureaucratic institutions;[8] or that he is taking up the themes of T. S. Eliot and other contemporary writers of the breakdown of theological institutions through the irrelevancy of their systems of communication between man and God.[9]

The fruitlessness of various allegorical interpretations of this irrelevancy, and of its concomitant futility, may result from the possibility that *The Trial* is concerned with the immanent irrelevancy which is characteristic of a contingent universe, and not with any specific examples of it; or it may be the result of the possibility that *The Trial* is not allegory at all. Both possibilities deserve examination, and such an examination may serve to open up the larger question of whether or not allegory is possible at all in a contingent world, regardless of the literary techniques.

Allegory may be defined as a literary device by which abstractions are represented by symbolic fictional figures who are presumed to have, or to bear, an analogy to "real life," or to "actual" moral facts. The distinction between allegory and apologue, or between allegory and fable, often made on the basis of the nature of the symbolic figure, is not a substantive one: the ability of a figure to function allegorically depends entirely upon its relationship to an analogue, and hence upon the acceptance by the reader of the existence of

[8] A good example of this point of view is presented by Edwin Berry Burgum, in Chapter 5 of *The Novel and the World's Dilemma*, New York: Oxford University Press, 1947.

[9] Instances of this point of view are legion. They may have had an initial impulse from Max Brod, whose personal relationship with Kafka gave to his criticisms a certain special weight. In particular, an outline of the dimensions of this frame of reference may be clearly seen in *Guilt*, by Francis Carryl Houselander (New York: Sheed and Ward, 1951) and in the studies of Anne Fremantle, such as "Kafka's Diaries" (*Commonweal*, L, [June 10, 1949] 227–228), and "Every Relationship Between God and Man But One" (*Commonweal*, LX, [April 30, 1954] 98–99).

a so-called "real" world outside the figure and outside the work. Another way to put it is to suggest that in allegory an image takes the place of a concept. This is true regardless of the method of the allegory, which is often relatively rigid and conventional, and it is also true of symbolism, where the "real" essence of a concept is contained within, and subsumed under, the particular sign. For this reason allegory and symbolism can function only in an environment in which there is a community of belief, a "real" world to which the symbols are referential. Let us suppose, however, that instead of dealing with concepts, Kafka is dealing only with situations, with conditions, which have no quality other than themselves, which cannot therefore be related to an analogous order. The metaphor, in such a construct, stands only for itself, and our attention is directed not to its external affiliations but to its internal structure. When we insist that the metaphor be metaphorical we come as far from appreciating its nature as does Joseph K. from appreciating his situation—the procedural flaw is the same. We are thus confronted in *The Trial*, (and in the larger percentage of Kafka's other writing) with a series of images which are frozen, and which have a curiously static quality. There is much in common in this confrontation with the experience of painting, in which we look upon an entire statement which, since it is a painting, is beyond the demands of chronology and hence does not lead us astray into trying, for example, to find out where it starts. Much criticism of painting, however, in making the same error with respect to the canvas that Joseph K. makes with respect to his circumstance, enquires into what the painting "means," insisting thereby on considering it as a metaphor of some external "reality," whereas it may only be itself. There is room in art criticism, however, for the recognition, if not the acceptance, of the point of view that a painting may not be referential, but may be only itself, because the form does not in itself make demands. An unhappy

33

woman in a painting may be unhappiness itself, not a sign of
it. Paintings may be conditions on canvas to which we can
react as we react to conditions elsewhere; but prose is in its
nature symbolic, "the empire," as Sartre expresses it, "of signs."
It is symbolic because language is symbolic and like all symbol,
it presupposes an analogous "reality," a referential universe.
Literary criticism is forever haunted by the quest for "meaning" which this aspect of literature provokes.

Man, however, may in fact be nothing but what he is. There
may only be situations, and if these situations are nothing more,
they are static and require to be painted, not "described." It
is here that Kafka has to face a fundamental technical problem, that of expressing static situations in a medium which by
its nature suggests movement and reference. He solves this,
to begin with, by making the metaphor "real," and by pre-
senting us with images of metaphors which have lost their
metaphorical significance (referential to an external "reality")
and become nothing more or less than themselves. It is an
inversion of the sequence, too often taken for granted, that
"experience" comes before the linguistic symbol which hence-
forth will refer to it, that a separation exists between the
conscious life of an individual and the language with which he
interprets and identifies it. What we are may, in other words,
be what we "say" we are, or at least what other people are
willing to "say" we are.[10] The quest for identity is therefore
bound up, not in an odyssey through a "world," but in a search
for linguistic authority to be something. The most common of
such authority is official documents, and official documents are
cast in official language. Language in general, and "officialese"
in particular, is all that a man cast out into a contingent
universe still retains of his humanity. Kafka insists upon the

[10] *Vide* Oliver Wendell Holmes' discussion of this problem in *The
Autocrat of the Breakfast-Table*, Boston and New York: Houghton-
Mifflin and Co., 1892. Vol. 1, 54.

external form of the symbol as such; he gives figures of speech, and associations, in their own right. The distinction between symbol and thing symbolized disappears, a corollary to the disappearance of the distinction between man and function.

The function of a man may be considered to have the same relationship to "him" as symbol has to thing symbolized—both function and symbol refer to something else and hence are distinct from it, dissimilar to it except associatively and referentially. Of the two parts which are distinct, the "something else" is the "real"; thus there is behind the function of a man an implied "real" man, or "true" man, who is seen as performing one function or another, and who consequently has the option of taking an attitude towards what he is doing and, presumably, of modifying or ceasing it when it fails to meet certain requirements held by "him." This is the world which Emerson assumes without question in his essays, especially in his *American Scholar*, where he recognizes that while men are distinguished one from the other by the functions which they perform in society, behind each function is the common state of being a man: the farmer is really "man farming"; the teacher, "man teaching"; and the scholar, "man thinking." There is, in short, a transcendental reality, of which individual functions or phenomena are representative. One of the characteristics, however, of the Kafkan universe, and one which has been increasingly impinging itself upon our own awareness of the nature of the world, is the loss of this distinction between man and his function. We are faced with a condition where the job and the man are in fact one, so that if the one is removed the other loses his identity. A man's profession becomes his exclusive existence, and he cannot be defined apart from it.

5 ·

Man, Function, and the Normative
Nature of Literature

It is the assumption of traditional fiction that the distinction between a man and his job not only exists, but that the job is in all cases subordinate. Thus the profession of a man is conceived as existing only outside the "real self" of the protagonist, who may have to it a number of variable reactions: he can see the profession as stifling him, he can see the profession as according with his views of the world, he can see the profession as making demands upon him which he will be compelled to satisfy or to ignore. Silas Lapham, for example, is a merchant and businessman, and within his commercial world he performs his various functions with sufficient skill to enable him to "rise" to financial success. At a certain point in *The Rise of Silas Lapham*, however, the "man" Lapham, who has always existed in the novel as the primary element, must decide, on the basis of his own moral code, whether or not to do something which is functionally efficient and proper within the business world which he inhabits. The fact that he decides to sacrifice his financial advantage to a moral one is itself of no importance except as a means of finding out something about what William Dean Howells may have thought of the priorities of values. What is important is that Lapham exists, and will continue to exist, apart from his function, so that he is able to view his function from outside and come to conclusions about it. In his *Guard of Honor*, to take a more recent example, James Gould Cozzens' character Colonel Ross, in reviewing the decisions which he has been called upon to make at a time when the stability of the military order

threatens to collapse, concludes that in protecting the particular
order of which he is a temporary part, he is acting in accordance with the values of his ordinary profession. He could,
had Cozzens so chosen, have come to the opposite conclusion:
the essential element is that there is a *person* able to evaluate
the function which he has been performing.

The sanctity of the *person* is therefore a critical element in
the way in which literature itself operates, for we understand
the actions of a protagonist as being, among other things, signs
of his rejection of what he might also have plausibly done.
His actions are in a sense "deviations" from a latent or implied
norm, or variations on the theme of plausibility. These variations, although they are manipulated by the act of writing, can
only be meaningful in terms of the factor which varies, and
that factor is of course the character himself. In order to be
able to vary, the character must have an existence apart from
what he does, and, in fact, the nature of this existence may
modify, in whole or in part, that which he does. That ambiguity
which is so much a part of the impact of tragedy, begins with
an ambiguity derived from the many levels on which a character has his existence. Clytemnestra is at one and the same time,
and in the natural order of things, woman, mother, wife, illicit
lover, queen. No given action which she takes can at the time
she takes it fail to be the action of all of these rôles. The ambiguity and, indeed, the conflict, stems from the fact that what
is appropriate to the one may be inappropriate to the other.
The matter is complicated by the fact that each level is not
simple, but has been given certain specific limitations: Clytemnestra is not just a woman, but a woman of certain characteristics; she is not just a mother, but the mother of a girl who
has been killed by her husband; she is not just a wife, but
the wife of a man who is himself at once king/leader and the
murderer of their daughter; she is not just mistress, but mistress
of a man whose title to the throne is far from clouded; she is

not just queen, but queen at a point where usurpation has occurred. Since no action is open to her in one capacity which is not an action in all the other capacities, she must choose, and in choosing, she will show herself not only as an example of the anguish of choice, but as the sponsor of a priority of values. This choice, so essential for the movement of the genre, is not possible unless there is somebody to make it. The character must have an existence apart from his function, to whatever degree he may be independent of it. Even when, in certain concepts of the universe, there is no choice which can be "right" or "successful"; when a man, perhaps because he is a man, can in effect do nothing which is not wrong, we appreciate his struggle, admire it, and hug it to us as token of the inviolable "dignity" of our condition. Oedipus is doomed, but we have for his refusal to admit his wrong entirely, for his continued crustiness when he arrives at Colonnus, for his flashes of temper, an admiration which in the course of time is even felt by the gods, whose instrumentality he becomes. We recognize the *person* as distinct from his function, and in this fashion we try, to a small extent at least, to ennoble the condition of man by removing it from the behavioristic world of responses to stimuli.

The actions within a work, then, imply the latent norm from which they are deviations and establish two bases from which traditional criticism, and traditional structure, proceed: (1) the actions require consideration because they vary from the implied norm; (2) they will in themselves constitute an explicit or implicit ascription of cause. This ascribed cause in turn reflects the author's view of the nature of human nature, or at least those aspects of it which he takes for granted, and by reflecting it in this fashion, within the fabric of the literary text, he postulates it as universal. The nature and configuration of the universality will vary, and can depend upon a relationship to generalizations within certain systematic formulations:

the psychological (in the sense both of Freudian method and merely the primacy of the psychological need and motive); the religious or theological in all their permutations; the societal; or it can be a figure of chance, contingency or happenstance. Both the implied norm and the postulations are understood by author and reader, not necessarily in their particular detail, but in the assumption that they exist and can therefore be discovered. The act of criticism is in many instances the application of a method designed to bring out this inherent kernel of "truth," this core of meaning, and the fact that many critics show a seemly modesty does not change the circumstance that they assume the kernel to be there even when they admit the inadequacy of their tools. For they must make this assumption when they are confronted with the structure of the literary experience itself. The assumption follows from the fact that the literary structure is based upon it. Any suggestion to the contrary is met with a great deal of disturbance: some worry lest Othello's occupation be gone; others respond by recoiling from what must be a void: "In that case. . . . . . ." Well, in that case we may be dealing with something else altogether.

The inherent configuration, in traditional literary movement, of the action as deviation from the implied norm serves as both purpose *and* device, and as a result governs the structure as well as the meaning. Critical analyses which are primarily concerned with meaning may hence miss the structural significance which underlies it, or may make the error of seeing the structure only as vehicle. But variations on the theme of plausibility require the presentation of stated responses to implied static stimuli, to which, at a minimum, an opposite response would have been equally acceptable. Thus the stated response is two things at once: it is positive statement and it is negative rejection of at least its inferential contrary; in short, *it is what it is* and it *is not* what it might have been. Since, however, we

39

are led by the mechanism of literature to understand what the response is in terms of what it might have been, we find it difficult to accept the proposition that *it is only what it is,* and that our insistence upon attributing part of its nature to what it is not (but might plausibly have been) is purely a function of two corollary attitudes and beliefs: that this is the method by which we apprehend the experience of literature and that this method, like literature itself, reflects a truth about the nature of the universe; that it is referential, not contingent, and that consequently actions, and of course the language in which they are conveyed, are symbolic, in some cases allegorical, in all cases allusive to a transcendental order of "reality." When, however, an action is nothing but what it is, it cannot be allusive, and hence the element of the literary structure which depends upon our understanding of the inherent allusiveness of action is no longer present. In this context, the "man" doing a job serves as the referential point of such allusiveness as we may wish to attribute to his actions. When the distinction between man and job has disappeared, and man has become nothing more or less than his profession, he cannot function symbolically, and he cannot for that reason function allegorically. He is no longer a sign of a condition but the condition itself, and the depiction of his condition thus takes on the qualities of painting, of images, of states. Since in literature this must be done through words, the metaphors must lose their metaphorical quality and retain only their face value. There is thus an internal inhibition upon the depiction of conditions as allegory, and even when, as in *The Trial*, the material seems to have the form of allegory, it can no more be allegory than can the legal system in which, because it has an older form, Joseph K. imagines himself to be embroiled. In both cases, analyses based upon this misapprehension will be futile. We have an example of criticism going astray for the same reasons that the protagonist himself goes astray—the work

Man, Function, and the Normative Nature of Literature

is seen by the critic as the world is seen by Joseph K., and neither is sufficiently aware of the possibility that he is dealing with reality rather than metaphor. We thus become aware of the general reaction to Kafka's writing as "obscure," an obscurity which is matched by the remoteness of the Law or of the Castle. But obscurity is the other side of clarity, and we tend therefore to clarify, or to try to clarify.

These clarifications, and attempts at clarifications, occupy not only a good deal of the time of the critics, but a good deal of Joseph K.'s time as well. Indeed, *The Trial* and *The Castle* are exercises in progressive efforts at clarification. We shall consider the particular nature of these efforts elsewhere. They are, of course, never going to be successful, for we are dealing with haecceity, which cannot really be understood except in its own terms. It does no good, for example, to conclude that the difficulty lies in the insistence by Kafka on making use of a private set of metaphors, which are simply more difficult to interpret because we cannot lean upon a well-known allegorical world, such as that of Christian theology. In doing so we may forget that in Kafka, literary convention and real condition have fused.

The matter of the immanent referential quality of the literary experience, the element which always prevents us from apprehending it as quiddity, may be illustrated from Act I, scene iii of *Othello*. It will be recalled that earlier Iago has informed Othello of the fact that Brabantio has spoken of him in "scurvy and provoking terms," that he has, in fact, called him, to his face, a "foul thief," and an "abuser of the world, a practiser of acts inhibited and out of warrant." Othello's conscience is clear, he has in no way seduced or mistreated Desdemona; his conduct has been "honorable." Under these circumstances it would be plausible for Othello to react to his appearance before the Venetian Senate with anger, indignation, intemperate language. When he appears, he says:

Most potent, grave and reverend signiors,
My very noble, and approv'd good masters,
That I have ta'en away this old man's daughter,
It is most true; true I have married her.
The very head and front of my offending
Hath this extent, no more. . . . . . . (76–81)

This speech is a statement of the character of Othello. It is noble, elevated and above all temperate and respectful, *not only* because of what it says and the tone in which it says it, but because it is at the same time *not* the sort of speech which it could just as well have been, and hence Othello is *not* the sort of man he might just as well be. It is fair, therefore, to come to certain conclusions about the values inherent in the character of Othello with respect to the meaning of the play and with respect to Shakespeare's hierarchy of values. The structure permits the lines to have signification on a number of different levels. We recognize that we are in the presence of allusiveness and react accordingly.

Another instance may be found in *Oedipus Rex*. At the beginning of the play, Oedipus is confronted with a petition that he find a means of delivering Thebes from the afflictions which the gods have visited upon it. He responds:

I grieve for you, my children. Believe me, I know
All that you desire of me, all that you suffer;
And while you suffer, none suffers more than I.
You have several griefs, each for himself;
But my heart bears the weight of my own, and yours
And all my people's sorrows. I am not asleep.
I weep; and walk through endless ways of thought.[11]

It would be plausible for Oedipus to have rejected the plea entirely, to have accepted the plea with ill grace, to suspect some hidden motive in the asking, to offer as a reason for

[11] The quotation is taken from the translation by E. F. Watling, published in 1947 by Penguin Books, Harmondsworth, Middlesex, England under the title *The Theban Plays*.

doing something the fact that it will relieve his own discomfort, but he does none of these. He makes a statement which, because it may be compared to the statements he might have made, serves to stand for the qualities not only of Oedipus himself, but the qualities which a "good king" should have, from which we may derive, once again, certain conclusions about the nature of kingship and responsibility in general, and in particular as these qualities are ranked in Sophocles' own hierarchy of values. Indeed, the "inner play" which has to do with Oedipus the king as opposed to Oedipus the man, moves forward only in these terms, as we realize when, later on, after hearing Creon's report of his conversation with Apollo, Oedipus states his firm decision to pursue the killer of Laius in these terms:

> You will find me as willing an ally as you could wish
> In the cause of God and our country. My own cause too—
> Not merely from a fellow-creature will I clear this taint,
> But from myself. The killer of Laius,
> Whoever he was, might think to turn his hand
> Against *me;* thus, serving Laius, I serve myself.[12]

Within the statement, of course, there is contained a motive, that of self-preservation, and as such the speech must be taken as indicating that Oedipus has this motive. Its significance within the play, however, is larger when it is compared with two things which it is not (and which it could plausibly have been): it contrasts with the attitude implied in Oedipus' earlier speech, cited above, and by that token embodies the fact of change (for which an explanation must be sought); and it is different from what it might have been (the attitude of a "good king"). For this reason, the speech also functions as the point in the play where the disintegration of Oedipus as king is first noticed, and if we are taken aback by the pit which this opens up for us, it is because we are already operating in a referential

---

[12] Watling translation, *supra.*

world of an order of kingship. We have thus, at the minimum, Oedipus as man and Oedipus as king: the one refers to an order of humanity, the other to an order of profession, and in an ideal universe the two would not conflict, or rather we would hope that there would never be a reason for them to conflict. In fact, since they are not the same, they do conflict, and we become aware of the anguish of the human condition, which is in a way a function of the distinction between man and job. Our apprehension of the play is thus dependent upon our unquestioned assumption of this distinction, which stands for the larger distinction between symbol and thing symbolized. Take this distinction away, place the action in a universe of contingency pure and simple, and the structure is no longer relevant. If we continue to try to reflect such a universe with an irrelevant structure, we will fail, as writers and as critics. But a structure is not relevant or irrelevant entirely in terms of its formal characteristics—it may retain formal characteristics from another order of ideas either because there are no new ones to take their place or because since any formal characteristic is irrelevant anyway, it does not make any difference. This is in part the burden of the argument offered by Dr. Huld, Joseph K.'s attorney. The ability of a given formal structure to relate to the "actual" is perhaps a question of the assumptions which we are prepared to make about it.

So-called artistic meaning, therefore, comes from the structure of the literary work itself, which suggests that the area of concern is invariably that which, if we consider the latent norm to be a straight line, would subtend the hypotenuse represented by the extreme limits of the deviation from that norm.

6.

Awareness and the Assimilation of Experience

There is another process which takes place in traditional literary structure, that of the assimilation of experience. As from outside the work, the reader/critic may be said to assimilate the experience of the work (that is, the significance of the totality of the work), so from inside the work the protagonist goes through the same process and assimilates the experience which involves him. In so doing, he expresses an awareness of his own internal relationships to the latent norms from which his conduct is structurally a deviation, and provides us with an opportunity of making a judgment, first of the degree to which he is aware at all, second of the perspicuity of his awareness. There thus is the "man," this time as functioning protagonist, and his rôle within the work, another dimension of the distinction of man and job in the "real" world. The disappearance of this distinction (as the result of its disappearance in the "real" world) makes the process of assimilation of experience from within the text impossible, for there is "nobody" to do the assimilating when that which would normally be assimilated, the "experience," is not distinct from the character, who is only what he does, and nothing more. Much of meaning, therefore, depends upon the ability of a literary structure to provide a means of conveying awareness, which in turn requires that "somebody" should exist who is capable of "being aware." Sartre makes this clear by offering a bipartite division within the individual of the *"pour soi"* and the *"en soi,"* roughly corresponding to "observer" and "thing observed," but its fundamentally ontological origin makes it only partially useful. It is in fact from the assimilation of experience from

45

within the text that redemption declares itself in tragedy, for there must be a distinction between the act and the doer before the doer can understand it, or accept his responsibility for it, or postulate the essential rightness of the order which his act contravened, and thereby allay the tragic qualm. When there is no awareness, there can be no tragedy, nor, indeed, referential relevance.

The necessity of awareness is not modified, reduced, or eliminated by the nature of the experience to which it directs itself. This experience may, in fact, be that of contingency as well as that of a world of *a priori* values. Its critical importance in the functioning of the literary process is nowhere clearer than in Shakespeare, and can be seen if we look at the assimilation of experience by Hamlet and Othello. Hamlet inhabits a world in which, since the collective reality of the social order can no longer be assumed or taken for granted, it is necessary to search for some definition of his own personal reality, to engage, in other words, upon a quest for his identity. In this respect he is placed, within the play, in at least the initial terms of the condition of Joseph K. at the opening of *The Trial*. But Hamlet is neither identical with his function/rôle/job nor is there evidence that the disappearance of the difference constitutes the estimate of the nature of ambiguity which Shakespeare makes. As a result, Hamlet sets about his search for identity with the presumption that he must seek it *because* it cannot be found in the collective reality about him, but with a corollary presumption that this does not imply that he has no identity at all, only that he will have to discover it through his own efforts. The shape that these efforts take reflects not a frenetic application of the *forms* of reason of the sort which leads Joseph K. to an unending series of frustrations, but the careful application of reason to an area of the problem which Hamlet has carefully delimited, and which he sets himself in consequence to explore. His quest for identity therefore takes the form of his considered examination of the relationships he has with the people who surround him, in both their "real" and their "assumed" personae, and constitutes, consequently, a deliberate program of testing the conditions in which he finds himself, subjecting them to rational analysis and rational evaluation. Nothing could be farther from despair, nothing could be farther from neurosis, nothing could be farther from irrelevancy and futility. In this fundamentally empirical program Hamlet has to come to grips with another level of ambiguity, more complex in a way than that level which inheres in the condition of being a human being who must in his own person play a number of diverse rôles in the normal course of affairs—he must try to achieve some sort of harmony among not only the diverse rôles as such, but the *estimates* of those rôles held by the persons playing them. This circumstance requires, of course, an understanding on the part of Hamlet that rôles may be "assumed" and not "real," and may hence vary from situation to situation rather than be immutable. He thus finds it incumbent upon him to consider, estimate, and weigh the particular passions which affect, in different degrees, the various persons with whom he comes into contact: the nature of the rôles they are *supposed* to play (in the apparent reality of the society which they inhabit) with respect to him; the nature of the feelings he is *supposed* to have towards them if he should play his reciprocal rôle; the feelings he actually has; and the feelings which he should demonstrate within his private, haecceitic world of values. The nature of Hamlet's discovery about the world would thus seem to be that people's rôles are not so much inherent as donned, and that they don them in proportion as they conclude that by so doing they will reinforce, confirm, and protect from external disaffirmation their cherished images of themselves.

This discovery of the nature of the world which Hamlet makes is carried further and into more complex ramifications

47

by *Othello*, where it would seem to include the realization that the passions of men can lead them to abandon rôles which are in their best interest and to assume, protect, and reinforce images of themselves which are false, and which will destroy rather than preserve them. This concept is not far, of course, from the concept of the destructive nature of passion in Greek tragedy, but it has this difference, that in Greek tragedy the destructiveness was held to come from the deleterious effects of passion upon the use of reason, which in turn was assumed to offer in itself a guide to "right" conduct, whereas in *Othello*, if we read the play in the light of Hamlet's discoveries, passion is destructive because it inhibits a particular application of reason, namely, to the act of choosing, with self-interest alone in mind, that rôle which will best strengthen the self-image. This is especially important in a universe in which no rôles exist other than those we choose. Within this order of ideas, the rôle of murderer is *assumed* by Othello (as all rôles are), and leads to the destruction of himself and Desdemona, because the passions of his hitherto suppressed impulses have operated to make it impossible for him to make a more careful choice with respect to his own best interests, and have caused him to make an incorrect evaluation of the courses open to him in the situation which he occupies. He makes, in other words, a serious mistake in judgment, of which the initial example in the play is his warm response to Iago's pretenses of friendship. Now these pretenses are no more pretenses than any other image which a person projects for his own purposes. Iago has assumed the rôle of "friend" because it suits him, not because he "is" a friend. Othello, whose only experience has been the simple one of war, and who does not have the soft parts of chamberers, fails to make a proper estimate of Iago because he is unaware of the nature in general of the rôle-making process. His failure is in his own limitations more than it is in any particular cleverness on the part of Iago, or of any particular "evil," which is why, in an earlier and perhaps more halcyon day, Iago's "malignity" was first of all taken for granted and then characterized as "motiveless." The irony of the situation inheres in the line "Haply for I am black"; if his blackness is the external symbol of that simplicity which makes the rôle-making process obscure to him, it is quite the opposite of "haply." As a matter of fact, he dies because he is. Hamlet would not make the same error.

But Othello is something more than the expression of a simple man, or than the expression of a man whose passions muddy his ability to estimate accurately the choices open to him—he is also noble, and this nobility gives two dimensions to his character which are never entirely resolved. It is from this duality of character that we get the extraordinary alternations within the play from elevation of sentiment to coarse vulgarity, from restraint to unleashed violence, from poetry to base prose, from the dignified to the bestial. And it is from this multi-sidedness of Shakespeare's characters that we get the possibility of choice which is open to them, which prevents them from becoming the abstract fusions of job and man which Kafka's characters are; which makes it possible for them to assimilate experience and to respond to it, and, indeed, to succeed in exhibiting, even in circumstances where their identity varies from situation to situation and their rôles vary accordingly, an astounding consistency, the totality of which is that comprehension of the world of which the genius of Shakespeare is made.

Shakespeare's characters hence change, and the degree and extent of their change relate to their ability to know themselves and to learn in the process about others. We are confronted with an excellent example in them of the *gain* of knowledge, and although the gain of knowledge is not directly connected to the nature of the knowledge gained, it implies none the less a basic motion of progress from one point to another, and it may be fairly assumed that the last of these points is the culmination of those which have led up to it. There is a cumulative effect, in other words, which makes the experience of the plays intelligible. It is, however, precisely this basic motion of progress which is missing in *The Trial*, and it is not only that as far as we can tell, Joseph K., *in propria persona*, does not progress, but the novel itself does not progress. We have suggested that in part this may be explicable in terms of considering the "episodes" as images alone, as series of states, and this is true from a technical point of view. It is also true, however, from another: there is in *The Trial* no gain of knowledge because there is no awareness, and there is no awareness precisely because job and man, person and function, are one—precisely for the same reason that makes the imagistic and still-life technique mandatory if this is to be conveyed. It is the fact of the gain of knowledge that offers to Shakespeare's characters, on the other hand, not only possibilities of choice, but true possibilities of choice, where no choice will be irrelevant and will fail to bring about the consequences inherent in it. For this reason, since we must consequently postulate the relevancy of all choices, we are on firm ground in recognizing that one of our important critical tasks is that of discovering the particular relevancy of a particular choice. Which is merely another way of saying that while we may not know exactly where Shakespeare is going, we know that he is on his way, so that Gray's warning, that we should not in reading Kafka but be concerned with what he is driving at, is not applicable to a reading of Shakespeare. Thus there is more than the gross difference which obviously exists between a novel by Kafka and a play by Shakespeare: they are qualitatively different, and we may be led astray if we apply to the reading of both, simply because they are both "literature," the same technical processes. We can become Joseph K.'s.

An interesting aspect of this problem of choice is that it makes it possible to understand what often appears as a contradiction, the fact that when consequences are inherent in the actions which bring them about, rather than imposed by some statutory authority from outside, the inevitability of the result suggests a determinism at variance with freedom of will, and thus further suggests, in embryonic outline, a pall of behaviorism. Dante illustrates the problem, because on the one hand the "sins" in *The Inferno* are existential in that they bear within them their own internal consequences, so that the "punishment" is not punishment at all but the living out in all eternity of the sin deprived of its metaphor (e.g., usury is a metaphor not for charging excessive interest but for the sterility which the reproduction of money implies, and for its falsification of the purpose of the reproductive processes in nature; hence the usurers sit in a sterile desert whose heat is only incidental), while on the other hand Dante is sensitively aware of the fact that there were possibilities of choice in the first place, so that while, the choice once made, the result is inevitable in the nature of things, in that same nature of things there was no absolute necessity that that choice be made. This belief gives to the work its own areas of deep compassion and makes it a noble estimate, in a way, of the human condition. In Kafka, on the other hand, there is not only the same depiction of the living out in permanence of a condition, which is both cause and effect in one, but the further statement that this condition was never within the realm open to choice at all, so that we are dealing not only with the view of man as behavior, but with the utter irrelevancy of any seeming choice which he may make. The place which man will occupy in the filing cabinet is set by the fact that he belongs in that place because of what he is, for the same reason that "Smith" and "Simpson" belong near each other because their names begin with S. He may be misfiled for a time, but he will be discovered, rooted out, and put where he belongs, until which time he may be ostensibly free. Jews did not choose to be Jews, but were Jews at the time that the Nazis killed them for being Jews. The consequence was inherent in the condition, but the condition was never subject to alternatives.[13]

The relativism of truth, or the conviction that its nature depends upon the angle from which you view it, is no less a "truth" about the nature of the world than the statement that truth is universal or immutable, but it has in literature a particular technical advantage in that it depends for its apprehension upon the aware observer, who not only "sees," but, while looking, compares what he sees with what he saw in another position and, indeed, is capable of making a further comparison with how he sees himself.[14] The confrontation

[13] Thus there developed in Germany various fruitless responses: indignation on the part of Jews who had been converted to Christianity because this external act seemed to have no essential relationship to the condition of which they were being accused; categories of half, quarter, eighth Jewishness, designed in a practical way to delimit the boundaries of the condition; the condemnation of persons who, although not in fact Jewish, were taken as being Jewish; as well as in the rest of the world, the curious series of statements of horror that Jewish children were slaughtered along with their parents, as if there were something worse about slaughtering certain Jews than about slaughtering others. As a matter of fact, the slaughter of "innocent" children was completely logical if we remember that they were not innocent of that of which they were accused, being Jewish. One of the horrors, and one of the sources of the success, of the Nazi state was that it put metaphor into practice and removed implication from conditions. We would be happier if the Nazi state fell for this reason, rather than merely from the application to it of superior military force. I am indebted for clarification of some of these ideas to Professor Rosalie L. Colie's paper, "Organizing the Final Solution: Patterns of Reaction," scheduled to appear in *Centennial Review*, XI (Summer, 1967).

[14] One of the reasons for the prevalence, in sadistic or masochistic individuals, of fantasies is that in these fantasies they are able to play a rôle in which they are both doer and observer. Many masochistic fantasies, for example, depend upon the ability of the individual to place himself in a position where he can see himself as the other person (the inflicter of punishment) sees him. He is both person *and* object. His masochistic pleasure is derived in part from becoming object; in fact, this is the source of humiliation. The widespread use of mirrors, in both solitary and collective sexual activity, to enhance the sexual pleasure, may be due to the convenience mirrors afford to those who wish to see themselves.

scene in *Troilus and Cressida* exemplifies this: what actually happens is that Troilus and Ulysses see Diomedes and Cressida seducing *and* being seduced. But all four are in turn watched by Thersites, and it is Thersites' ranting which serves to place the scene in the least honorable context, a context which it does not in itself contain. The meaning of "seduction," and the conclusions about it to which we may come, is effectively modified by each of the five characters according to his individual perspective, and there could conceivably be more. Troilus, for example, has at least two Cressidas, Diomedes' and his own, and one of the reasons he is able to maintain his sanity is that as a result he knows he is in a bipartite universe in which the allusive quality of actions, and their referential significance, have been retained. It is clear that none of this would be possible if the characters were incapable of assimilating experience because of an unawareness stemming from their being conditions rather than men.

Lack of awareness can, in the customary constructs of the world, come simply from ignorance (which in turn can be invincible), or be the product of a disadvantageous environment, an unfortunate genetic heritage, a disease, or the operation upon the mind of neurotic factors too strong to allow of the fullest potential play. In such cases the inability of the protagonist to understand becomes a statement of this inability, seen in contradistinction to his potential ability to understand, and hence functions as a signpost to the cause of the inability and even as a possible call to action to make such inability impossible in the future. Lack of awareness, however, can also be the result of the circumstance that there is nothing to be aware of, since the individual may be only a condition and not distinguishable from that condition. That this is a persistent theme in contemporary writing may be suggested by Beckett's *Endgame*, in which the representation of unawareness is reduced to its ultimate point and the characters *are* ashcans, not persons who for some reason which the play will presumably make clear towards the end have found themselves in ashcans, or have chosen ashcans as a home, or a refuge. In Kafka's *In The Penal Colony* the point is clearer. The condemned man is in a situation which traditionally consisted of punishment and acceptance of the justice of the punishment through an awareness on the part of the condemned that: (1) the act for which he is being punished is in fact a crime, or a sin; (2) it is right that he die in order to justify the order of the moral universe to those who come after him—in brief, redemption. The extreme complication of the execution machine, far from being a device to excite sadistic interests, is a function of this redemptive purpose, in that the death of the condemned is delayed long enough to make it possible for him to have an awareness of its significance, and the nature of the sin is apprehended not through the possibly superficial medium of words, but in the flesh itself. The pain is incidental; the ritual has meaning in terms of its own order. But the condemned man in the story is too stupid in any case to be able to understand anything, and certainly too stupid to be able to understand the redemptive qualities of his punishment. Indeed, if he is to "read" the nature of his sin in the letters which the harrow draws upon the flesh of his back, he must be able to read, and he is clearly illiterate to begin with. He thus "is" unawareness, not a symbol of it, and as "unawareness" he is not going to be able to function within an entire system which is predicated upon awareness—that is, he will not be able to assimilate his experience, and as a result, neither will we. Moreover, the crime for which he is being punished, that of having failed to obey his superiors, has in itself become reduced to form. The condemned man has failed to salute the door, at periodic intervals, behind which his superior officer was sleeping. If we assume that the ignorance of the condemned man, his illiteracy, is the opposite of the plausible possibility that he be literate, and that hence the system is destroyed by the

ignorance of its victim alone, we can salvage the possibility
that it could be maintained if ignorance were to be avoided:
in other words, that the system has collapsed because of a
situation which is in theory remediable, in which case Kafka
might be held to have made some sort of potentially valuable
"statement" about things. But even if the condemned man
were literate, there is nothing to read, so that the absence of
values and the ignorance of the condemned man both function
to make awareness impossible, and thus bring about the utter
collapse, with great clanking, of the system which is based
upon awareness. For the man who cannot face this, immola-
tion is of course the most useful answer, and the officer dies
in the debris of his apparatus.

The process, therefore, by which the reader derives the
"meaning" of a work, in a limited way or in a larger context
of universal values, is through the assimilation of experience
by the protagonist within the text. This assimilation in turn
implies that there is an experience to be assimilated, and an
awareness of it.

7 .

Meaninglessness and Choice

One difficulty arises in that as, in late years, it has been borne
in on many writers that existence may be meaningless, meaninglessness has simply been substituted for the meaningfulness
which older literary works assumed and attempted to adum-
brate. First of all, it is necessary to be aware that life is
meaningless before the meaninglessness of life can be the proper

subject of literary treatment, so that two aspects of traditional literature are retained despite the seeming reversal of the conclusions: (1) awareness remains, and there is a distinction between man and rôle; (2) meaninglessness takes on its significance because we understand it as the opposite of the more plausible meaningfulness. *Plus*, in other words, *ça a semblé changer, plus c'est la même chose.* Much of modern literature is thus, in a manner of speaking, a kind of hat trick, in which the fact that it still reflects the older order of the universe is concealed by its apparent iconoclastic concern with the death of the old order. But the next level after the statement that meaninglessness is tragic is awareness of the tragedy of meaninglessness, and this is handled in two general ways: the meaninglessness of actions is unrelated to the nature of the person engaged in them (*vide* Robert Jordan in Hemingway's *For Whom the Bell Tolls*) and is hence "general"; or it is a direct function of the nature of the individual (*vide* Clyde Griffiths in Dreiser's *An American Tragedy*). In both cases, however, it is a statement about meaninglessness, not meaninglessness itself, and various ways of handling this phenomenon are implied or may be derived.

Kafka does none of these things. His presentation of the nature of experience takes on its apposition to a contingent universe because his characters *are* their conditions, not signs of them. He does not write allegory, and not because he writes "non-allegory," but because allegory is impossible within his terms.[15]

---

[15] That Kafka is writing allegory seems often to be a matter of faith. In referring to the fusion of the mental and physical in Kafka's work, for example, R. O. C. Winkler says that this fusion "is the basis of his allegorical method." ("The Novels," *Scrutiny*, VII: 3, 1938) He apparently does not doubt for a minute that he is dealing with allegory. This assumption may stem in part from the recognition of certain symbolic attributes which some of the names of Kafka's characters seem to bear: Frieda (peace); Bürgel (diminutive of Bürge, guarantor); Landvermessen, K.'s profession in *The Castle,* with its allusions to

Meaninglessness and Choice

His characters are abstractions, removed from a real world to which they are trying to return; they are the metaphorical constituents of the linguistic metaphors, struggling back to their verbal homes. The world from which they have been torn is the world in which the distinction between man and his job still exists; the sign of their exile is the fact that they have become only their jobs. *The Trial* has a *dramatis occupationes* rather than a *dramatis personae*.[16]

The difficulty of comprehending the disappearance of the distinction between man and his job is as great in literary analysis as it is great in the world we inhabit. In both contexts the critical faculty tends to boggle and, having boggled, to recoil. The trial of Eichmann in Israel was, as an example, a vain effort to bring monstrosity into reasonable focus, to complete a dossier by the careful enumeration of monstrous acts with the evident implication that the full degree of Eichmann's bestiality would be apparent as the instances multiplied. In short, Eichmann's crime was seen: (1) as a crime of the sort which is normally to be found in any society; (2) as a greater (more serious) crime because of the scale on which it was committed. Monstrosity was thus defined as crime, but on a

---

Vermessenheit (hubris) and sich vermessen (to commit an act of spiritual pride). But these allusions in themselves would hardly make of Kafka's work a true allegory. They are at best the *form* of allegory, and not even an essential one at that. For further examples, and an elaboration of this approach, *vide* Erich Heller, "The World of Franz Kafka," in his *The Disinherited Mind*, New York: Farrar, Straus and Cudahy, 1957.

16 This is one of the reasons why it is hard to understand the bland ease with which critics such as René Dauvin interpret the Court as representing the Synagogue of Prague, or say of it: "The Divine Law is unknown and the Court has lost its key, for God is the creator and keeper of moral values." ("*The Trial*: Its Meaning," in Flores and Swander, *Franz Kafka Today*, Madison: University of Wisconsin Press, 1958, p. 149.) This interpretation suggests the desirability of a sign in front of the entrance to the Court: "Pour clef, s'adresser au concierge Dauvin."

larger scale in that it resided not so much in the nature of any individual act as in the magnitude of their cumulation. The defense of Eichmann was his constant iteration that he had been doing nothing more or less than his "job"—that on many occasions when his "job" compelled him to do things, or to witness events of a particularly brutal nature, he himself was repelled. Indeed, Eichmann testified constantly to the fact that he had nothing against the Jews, that he did not especially dislike them and that he had had many fruitful relationships with them. Some of his best victims were Jews, as a matter of fact. He did not have an obsessive interest in seeing to it that Jews were extirpated as a goal with its own values. On the contrary, he would have been willing to exchange his prisoners for other more valuable matériel, such as trucks, if the Allies had found the price right. But he had his "job" to do, and failure to do it would have meant his own execution, which naturally he could not be expected to invite. Nor was he in a position to know what reason underlay the decision of the authorities to place him in that "job"; there must have been a good reason or they never would have done so, and further-more it was not within his power to see, or within his discretion to question, the nature of the grand design. Within his "job," however, he could rightly be concerned with those variations of detail which were bound to occur: schedules could go awry, railroad cars could become delayed, and in some cases the victims themselves, by refusing to cooperate, could cause a number of difficulties which would try anybody.

It is hard, as we have said, to comprehend the nature of this situation in common terms because we cannot avoid the assumption that behind these actions there was a "man" who, since he had a potential of choice, chose to do what other "men" would not have chosen, and represented, in consequence, "evil" which could be defined, examined, explored and ultimately punished in a condign way. But Kafka, if we read him in this light, suggests that there was no "Eichmann" distinct from what Eichmann did. He was and remained only his function.

"I am here to whip people," says the Whipper in *The Trial*, "and whip them I shall." He is not a man who, whipping as a job, can conceivably be reached and, if the appeal be right, dissuaded from his work. Joseph K.'s attempt at bribery does not fail because the "man" behind the Whipper is opposed to bribes as a matter of principle. He cannot be dissuaded because he does not exist when his function ceases. To ask him to stop whipping is to ask him in effect to destroy himself. Within his orbit, however, he can make a certain number of discriminations: he notices that Willem is fat but immediately converts this observation into functional terms. "See how fat he is," he says to K., not, as such a remark would ordinarily operate, to call attention to one of the more common variations of the human person, but to introduce the next expert opinion that "the first cuts of the birch will be quite lost in fat." Willem is object, not man, and is seen only in relation to the job of whipping him.

K., it would appear, is horrified, but what causes him the greatest anguish is the shriek which Franz lets out when the whip descends upon his flesh, a shriek which "did not seem to come from a human being but from some tortured instrument, the whole corridor rang with it, the whole building must hear it." But this is far from empathetic concern, for K. does not flinch in identification with the tortured Franz; rather, he is horrified lest the noise bring the situation to the attention of the other people in the bank, lest some clerk, finding him involved in such a scene, might think ill of him; briefly, lest the image of himself which K. wishes to promulgate be jeopardized, thus jeopardizing K.'s own position and thus putting in peril his own job. Without realizing it, K. reacts as if in fact he were not distinct from his job, but his futility may be the result of his insisting, in his rational mind, upon acting as if he were. His rational mind then, instead of addressing itself to the possibility that he and his function are one, conceives a form of "guilt": that he had not succeeded in getting Franz excused from his whipping, which implies, of course, that he has reason, by allusion to some external standard, to think that it would have been "right" for him to do so, either because it is "right" to alleviate pain or because Franz did not "deserve" his whipping, since he had really "done nothing wrong" and would not have found himself in the punishment room if K. himself had not made a complaint in the first place. The truth is, however, that K. does not really understand, nor does he attempt to explore, the meaning, nature or ramifications of this "guilt," because it is not guilt at all, but simply a residual, vestigial feeling of guilt, left over from another time and another order when such situations in fact produced substantive guilt. The reaction he has, and which he dresses in the linguistic raiment of guilt, is fear of the loss of his identity through loss of his job, and his mind betrays this when it engages in a rationalization of his conduct:

> He was deeply disappointed that he had not been able to prevent the whipping, but it was not his fault that he had not succeeded; if Franz had not shrieked—it must have been very painful certainly, but in a crisis one must control oneself—if he had not shrieked, then K., in all probability at least, would have found some other means of persuading the Whipper.

Thus his "guilt" is not guilt at all, but the fault of Franz, who did not play his rôle of victim properly. He had an obligation to receive the cut of the lash without making so much noise; he is the receiver of pain in the same way that the Whipper is the inflicter; he and the Whipper play reciprocal parts, and so long as they play them, there can be no disturbance. These rôles are inherent: "a man with a belly like that couldn't ever become a Whipper, it's quite out of the question," says the

Whipper when Willem first undresses. "There are Whippers just like me," maintains Willem, to which the Whipper responds with a "No" and a cut of the whip. The shriek of Franz, as K. sees it, makes any intervention impossible, because he "could not afford to let the dispatch clerks and possibly all sorts of other people arrive and surprise him in a scene with these creatures in the lumber-room." Such a conclusion would, in K.'s thinking, constitute too great a "sacrifice."

Much of this is lost if we consider, as many did when *The Trial* first appeared, the conduct of the Whipper to be representative of sadism, and the inclusion of the scene to indicate a need to analyze the psychological motivations of the author. It is the seeming absence of moral conscience, in the literary figure of the Whipper and in the actual figure of Eichmann, which the traditional modes of interpreting reality make us reject almost out of hand and hence seek to establish a dossier. If the order in which we live is the order of Eichmann, no novel can issue from this order other than that which *The Trial* exemplifies: no attempt to read as if there were moral conscience can do other than falsify analyses of figures who have become abstracted from the warp of conscience altogether; Joseph K. is not a man of conscience wandering in a world in which conscience no longer exists, but is in fact only another man/cum/function; what is left to him is only the skeleton of the language of rational thought, and he must apply this, ultimately, to no avail. Like Joseph K., Kafka himself may have been man/cum/function, that of expressing what he was able to express, "les aspects horribles et sans signification de la vie. . . . Tel était sans doute le mandat qui lui était donné. . . . et il fallait que, dans l'ombre, il travaillât à la projection de ses ombres, de ses fantômes, *lui fantôme*." (italics added)[17]

---

[17] Jean Wahl, *Esquisse pour une histoire de l'existentialisme*, Paris: L'Arche, 1949, pp. 148–149.

8.

Style and Language

When and if man becomes indistinguishable from his job, he can have no existence apart from that instrument which appoints him, of which he becomes what is in effect an official copy. In the absence of an original document to which he corresponds, he becomes what in the Soviet Union has come to be known as a "non-person"; he is in fact socially non-existent. "Compared with these documents, which are the token of his reality in the administrative world, the individual. . . . is as valueless as the actual phenomenon compared with its Platonic Idea."[18] He is therefore not only led to seek the documents if he does not have them, but he is led to engage in an endless quest for meaning in which no piece of evidence is too trivial to be ignored, too insignificant to be turned this way and that in order to extract from it its fullest possible bearing. The goal is that of returning to the world from which he has been exiled, the world of authorized functions. In *The Castle*, K. wishes not so much to *be* land-surveyor as to *be confirmed* as land-surveyor; it is a question of having clear title to life. A cloud upon the title is a death warrant.

For this reason Joseph K., and the majority of Kafka's characters, are in the position of standing outside a world to which they in effect seek admission. They are outsiders and hence petitioners, and they speak the language of petition. Peti-

[18] Günther Anders, *Franz Kafka*, New York: Hillary House Publishers Ltd., 1960, p. 49. Anders' view of Kafka, incidentally, which touched on the sensitive question of German guilt, angered Max Brod, who accused him of "misinterpretation" in his "Die Ermördung einer Puppe namens Franz Kafka. Replik." (In *Franz Kafka, eine biographie*, 1937).

tion is more than a request; it is request couched in an official form which reflects meet consideration of its two basic elements: (1) that the petitioner is inferior and subject to the power which is being petitioned; (2) that it is a formal, hence an unusual, form of address which is the only form of address the power can, or will ever be willing to, accept. In fact, it is the language of the power and represents a kind of concession to the petitioner, who in those special circumstances only, and for a limited period of time, and without any certainty of a favorable result, nor any assurance that the language will even be heard, may employ it. In any case, no other form of language would have any chance whatsoever of being listened to. The power thus tells the subject, "Don't come to me with your request phrased as you wish, in your own speech. Come, if you must come, and talk to me in *my* language, which, since you are incapable of knowing it as a living means of communication, you can use in the limited sense of the formal patterns." It is the ape as "party of the first part." Petition also implies a strong possibility that it will not be granted, so that the petitioner has the feeling, to a greater or lesser extent, that he has been rejected before his petition has even been filed. To reduce this feeling he may not only request, but may beseech and, to be certain, also implore. Hysteria is not far away, for so much depends upon the petition, and there is no way in which it can be controlled—the hope is that on the one level on which the petitioner is allowed to operate, that of formulating the petition, the language has been correct.

Language thus becomes critical. It becomes once again, to the adult seeking authorization to live, what it was to the child seeking a means of living, a way of manipulating the universe. Since the ability of language to manipulate the universe depends upon the validity of its referents, it must, so to speak, "work," and it can only work when the symbols which it uses are understood by others, and when they refer to a stable order of "reality." Language thus carries within it a number of assumptions, about relationships, about priorities, about structures; and it is corollary to the world of which it is an instrument of control. The language of *The Trial*, the language of petition, is thus an "official" language, a language which we would be tempted to call "legal" in its form and tone. We recognize this language as "legal" precisely because we recognize the difference between it and the customary language of the society. As a result, to the petitioner, who may use the language as a concession but who may not use any other, and to the reader, who is also at a remove from the courts, it has a certain "style." The degree to which it is apprehended as having "style" varies directly with the distance between the user and the world of law. To those who live in the world of law, legal language is not special, but normal. There is thus, between the petitioner and the official petitioned, at least this minimum difference, that while they both use the same language, they have towards it different attitudes. In the one case, the language has become a form of prayer, a formula through the proper use of which it is hoped that remote power may be moved to act in a favorable way; in the other, it is the only language which is feasible and valid. These differences of attitude are concealed because they are not reflected in the formal language itself—both the petitioner and the official petitioned *seem* to be using the same linguistic structures, and hence it is easy to fall into the assumption that they are in fact the same. In the one case, however, as Joseph K. soon discovers, there is no necessary correlation between the language and what it is presumed to refer to, so that it fails in its primary object, that of rational manipulation of the world, leaving him with no alternative but despair and the reiteration of the same formulas. The "complicated, precise formulae [of the law] have the external qualities of theoretical thinking, lacking only the most essential one—they don't illuminate reality, since what is 'given' is not the conditions of life, but merely a narrow convention."[19] In the other case, of course, it makes the efforts of Joseph K. appear puerile: as the tall warder says in Chapter I, he is behaving "worse than a child."

An additional consequence of this use of legal language as the "style" of the novel is that it makes impossible any distinctions in tone. Everybody in *The Trial*, high or low, uses the same language. It is virtually uniform, and this uniformity makes for monotony, which in turn is one of the sources of the sensation of fatigue which permeates the novel and which is shared by the reader and Joseph K. himself. The "legal" language of *The Trial*, the "officialese" in which it is written, has the function of holy idiom. And it is copious idiom as well, which fatigues by its surfeit. It is the traditional linguistic form in which man communicates with God, and performs, in a universe where God may be dead, or where the true power lies in the realm of administration where patents to live are granted, the same service. It is thus no more possible for Kafka to write *The Trial* in another "style" than it is possible for a traditional work of Christian theological concern to be written in other than "religious" language.

This language of *The Trial* has "the frightening precision of official notices," the complicated and all-inclusive structures which are "threatening reminders that ignorance of the law is no excuse."[20] But it serves also as an example of what may be called "immanent style," as opposed to gratuitous, or arbitrary style. For this particular "officialese" is not chosen by Kafka from among a number of styles available to him but is the only style in which the nature of his universe could be conveyed. If man stands to the world in the relationship of petitioner, he can only petition. If he can only petition, he is

[19] Dwight Macdonald, "By Cozzens Possessed," *Commentary*, XXV (January 1958), 41.
[20] Günther Anders, *op. cit.*, p. 69.

compelled to do so in the language of petition. The language of petition is not discrete from the petition itself. Another way to put it is to submit that there are no petitions which are not written in the language of petition, nor any language of petition which is contained in anything other than petitions. It is the *state* of being petitioner (a condition which is the result of the "actual" position of man with respect to the universe he inhabits) which controls the language in which this state is to be conveyed, not the independent and arbitrary choice of the writer. Thus the language creates its own large figure, of which the Court is the clearest example—the figure demands its own figurative language. In addition, this figure contains within it not only the state of the protagonist, but the *process* of the protagonist: the fact that "trial" and "process" are synonymous is not accidental. The language is demarcated in part by its all-inclusiveness, by its painful elaborations of all possible alternatives, by its effort to define inclusively and to leave no possibility out. That this is necessary in the language of statute derives from the nature of statute. It is a classification in advance of acts which have not yet been committed, and of persons who have not yet committed them. It relates not to the present of the statutory enactment, but to the future. It concerns not reality but a wishful statement about reality. It comes into operation only if and when certain preconditions have been met, and while it is supposed likely that they will be met, because they have had a tendency to be met in the past, it is not certain that they will be met at all, and it is conceivable that a statute may never have to be put to any classificatory test in a so-called trial. Statutes thus, in their nature, examine conditions, to the best ability of their framers and from every conceivable point of view, and in so doing, embody that ambiguity which is inherent in any diversity of view. One way of regarding a situation is balanced by another—each major class is subdivided into smaller ones; each precondition depends upon other preconditions; each inclusion implies an exclusion—until the situation which the statute is designed to control is subjected not to a single, but to a multiple series of examinations. The effort of the language to include these many points of view presupposes the ambiguity of experience. It is not language which treats ambiguity as a subject, nor is it designed to convey it: it is ambiguity itself, as closely related, one to the other, as petition to the language of petition. It is in this sense that both the large figure of *The Trial* and the language in which the novel is written are not only inextricable, but inevitable.

The "stylistic" quality of *The Trial* (and, indeed, of Kafka's other works) impinges itself upon us as "stylistic" quality not because, as we may think, Kafka has arbitrarily chosen to write in that manner, but because we become aware of what we call "style" under special circumstances. The style is really not style, but immanent. It seems to be style for the reason that, within the text itself, the condition of Joseph K. with respect to his relationship to the Court (and hence to the universe) is that of great distance, and awareness of style is a function of the appreciation of distance, first between the language used and the language habitually used; second, in the aesthetic distance which is maintained between two textual conditions. What we then think of as "beauty," in literature and in life, has to do with its remoteness, its unattainability, its assumed inviolability, in short, its distance from us—a distance which, since we find it convenient to associate the "greater" with the "higher," we find it useful to conceive in terms of "elevation," or "nobility." Style is thus altitude. Beauty of style derives from "elevation" of language above the ordinary usage.

The "beauty" which inheres in the remote is reflected in the terms which customarily refer to it: God is "beautiful"; sainthood represents "beatification"; the king is "sublime"; Heaven is conceived as the supremely beautiful place; and a woman such as the Virgin Mary is "beautiful" in proportion as her parthenogenetic idiosyncracies remove her from the ordinary— because of her ability to conceive a child without the prior help of a man, she has not been, nor ever will be, attained or violated. Some of the beauty which we associate with the Petrarchan sonnet is the result of the remoteness of the object of the poet's love, seen in this case not so much in terms of a description of the object *qua* object, but through the treatment of the position of the lover with respect to it. He is a lover without hope, miserable at the coldness of the woman, who submits himself to her caprices, who either cannot or will not put a stop to his adoration of her "beauty," and who in addition suffers from not being loved or, at least, from not having any tangible proofs of love. In this situation, the beauty of the loved one is not inherent, but originates in the image the lover has of himself. The conversion of self from subject to object which is the basic component of masochism is perfectly obvious. The victim, within this context, can attribute "beauty" to his torturer because his rôle of victim, and his concomitant abasement, places the torturer in a position of remoteness.

This aesthetic distance in literature, from which concepts of beauty and style are derived, has the analogue in the human world of social distance, marked by differences in social class and hence reflective of relationships of power. The attribute of power which distinguishes the powerful also creates between them and the powerless an intrinsic gap. We may say that the extent of this gap varies with the amount of power and hence with the degree of powerlessness. The source of power thus quickly lends itself to conceptions of remoteness, carried most easily in figures of altitude. The king becomes "le Roi Soleil" or, as in the case of the Japanese Emperor prior to World War II, so remote that he cannot even be seen or touched. Power becomes "majesty," "all-high," and in consequence is addressed in suitable language, which, because it differs markedly from the habitual usage, is converted in its apprehension into "style," or "elevation." It is interesting in this connection to note that "style," or "elevated" language, most often, in consequence of its nature, associated with stratified social orders, and hence with classicism, comes under fire at those points in history when egalitarian doctrines are in the ascendant. In political terms "style" may be reactionary, and for this reason concern with "beauty" is associated with a reactionary view, often expressed by the use of "artificial" as a pejorative adjective.

The difficulty in approaching the question of Kafka's style lies in the fact that, since there is an enormous distance between the protagonist and his goal, and since in addition he is powerless with respect to the power which he tries to confront, we have reason to expect a "style" which, reflecting this distance and this relationship, will be characterized by a form of "elevation." We find on the contrary that the "style" is quite the reverse: it is subjacent to the world it reflects, not elevated above it, so that it is the reverse of "noble," indeed the reverse of style altogether. Its relationship to ordinary usage is that of being more plain, more sober, more uninflected, not less so, and by this attribute it serves not to lift the reader out of ordinary experience by raising him above it, but to disengage the reader from ordinary experience by depressing him below it. The aesthetic result, interestingly, is the same, and we are no less aware of the fact that Kafka writes in a certain way than we would be if he had written conventionally.

This is more, however, than an arbitrary act of stylistic choice. It is implicit in the condition of the protagonist, Joseph K., who, having been rejected by the administrative world from which his authorization to function, and hence to live, emanates, is in the position of struggling to go back to where he was, of struggling to gain admission to a world from which he has been expelled. In this sense his progress forward cannot be progress upward, since it starts at a point below the one he occupied previously. The *status quo ante* thus becomes the goal, but if we assume for a moment that the *status quo ante* were ever attained, it would not really represent any progress. It thus becomes a critical concern, in the universe which Kafka postulates, to maintain one's footing at all—far from hoping to move upward and onward, one has to hope with desperation that one may be able to regain ground already lost. In this manner the present plays the rôle which the future plays in traditional religion, and in consequence an existential inversion of the traditional procedural relationships ensues.

For traditionally, man bound up in the terrestrial world knows, or seeks, a transcendental world beyond, a so-called "paradise" which he hopes to be able to attain in the future. This "paradise" is by definition in the future, so that all progress towards it is forward progress and, if the "paradise" be conceived in terms of conceptual altitude, upward progress. It is this which gives to traditional religious conceptions an inherent characteristic of optimism, of hopefulness, which is independent of the actual estimate of the possibility of gaining the goal. This optimism is reversed by Kafka, not because of a philosophically pessimistic estimate of man's chances of succeeding, but because of the empirical nature of the alienation of man with which he is concerned. Man in Kafka is alienated, and stands outside the world which he wants to enter, not because he has not yet entered it, but because he has been rejected by it. What he desires most acutely is to regain his identity, to be allowed to live. The relationships of the points remain integral, but the points of departure have shifted. As a result, the humdrum, the commonplace, the quotidian, the daily round of the actual and present world take on the aspect of the "beyond," of "paradise" in the world of orthodox religion, and indeed play the same part. Now if we recall that traditional literature, written out of an assumed orthodoxy, adopts the "style" of its immanent goal (which is "elevated" to the extent that the goal is high), the style of Kafka must necessarily be that of the immanent goal within his works, and that goal is the ordinary. The language is hence ordinary, and its ordinariness is emphasized by the circumstance that it is used to convey events which we consider as extraordinary: the face of horror is revealed as lying beneath the regular round of human existence, not beneath aberrant situations, and the monstrosity of evil is conveyed through the medium of its tidy presentation in documented, formal and neat language, that of the dossier. In short, the "actual" world is the world to come. Alienation, so central a theme in contemporary writing, is thus in Kafka more than a statement about the nature of man. It is the presentation of the condition of alienation and a much more extended version of it. Alienation is a thread which runs through the structure, and which informs it: as the metaphor has lost its metaphorical aspect and become literal, so has alienation lost its referential quality to the specific terms of the estrangement. They can be those of God, or of the society of man, or of the self, or of tradition, but is of no matter; we are confronted with the anatomy of the outsider.

PART II

9.

The Inversion and Suspension of Time

Style, of course, cannot be distinguished from other factors, such as those of movement, and the style of Kafka produces, as we have noted before, a sense of fatigue. It is material that this sense of fatigue is a corollary to the fatigue which Joseph K. himself feels. It is weariness conveyed in the garb of weariness; but it is also something else, for part of the fatigue is inherent in the frustration of the need for arrival. The feeling that one is going somewhere is bound up in the feeling that at some point in the future one will arrive—forward movement contains the concept of arrival. It is difficult, however, to "arrive" if one is going to the point of departure: there is no satisfactory antonym for the verb "arrive," but if there were, *The Trial* would be its configuration in literary form. We have the inversion of ordinary movement, and hence the inversion of time, which no longer plays a substantive part in the development of the novel. The paralysis of time is what gives the feeling of a series of static images, which have no chronological relationship to each other, and it is the paralysis of time in the novel which is the complement of the paralysis of the protagonist. The scene in which the warders are being whipped, for example, resumes whenever Joseph K. opens the door to the lumber-room, and presumably ceases when he closes it. It goes on outside of time and has chronology only in terms of the act of viewing it, like a continuous movie which "begins" when we enter the theater and "ends" when we leave. For that reason, the order of the chapters is unimportant:[1] they

[1] *Cf*. Footnote 24, Introduction.

all could be rearranged without injury to the totality of the textual experience and (as happened with respect to *The Castle*) could be continued indefinitely.

A more precise definition of futility thus emerges. It is the futility which characterizes repetitive behavior, and behavior becomes purely repetitive when it has been deprived of anticipation. So soon as "arrival" is ruled out, anticipation must disappear. Arrival in *The Trial* is ruled out, first, because one cannot arrive where one has already been, and second, because the protagonist is never going to be able to "arrive" in the world because he does not belong there in any case. He is doomed actually and structurally. Now if the "actual" has the attributes of the "beyond," it is not possible for the protagonist to inhabit it, and this requires, for purely literary reasons, the suspension of time which, as we have seen, is also the source of the sense of fatigue and the conviction of futility. To represent a character who cannot "arrive," it is necessary to suspend that aspect of the character which is connected with the act of arriving, his movement. Since movement takes place in time, it can best be arrested by suspending time, and time may best be suspended by arresting the character. Joseph K., of course, is in fact arrested, and his arrest may mean this rather than all the possibilities which he pursues. The arrest of the character has the effect of placing him in a sort of limbo between the past and the future, a limbo in which he is confronted exclusively either by events which have already occurred (*vide* the whipping scene or the initial visit of the warders) or by events which are going to take place (the progress of his affidavits, his case, and his eventual death). He is never confronted with what is actually going on because what is actually going on is beyond him, figuratively and actually. For him, the present is unattainable. In such a limbo it follows that no effort he makes to handle his environment can be effective, by reason of his delusion that he is in the

73

present when in fact he is not. The theme of irrelevancy which permeates the novel may, as we have already discussed, have its own implications, but the inherent irrelevancy of the novel comes from its structure, a structure in which the protagonist does not occupy the point in time which he thinks he does. It is not surprising that he fails when he tries the hardest, nor that he succeeds when he makes an involuntary or irrelevant gesture. Furthermore, the suspension of the possibility of "arriving" sometimes takes the form of arriving too late. A late arrival is no arrival at all, but only has the form. There is nothing more futile, or less substantive to effective action, than arrival at a train station after the train has left, but Kafka's heroes often, with great puffing, do just that.[2] Irrelevantly finding the law courts, in Chapter II, by asking for the whereabouts of an invented character called Lanz, Joseph K. is greeted by an angry magistrate whose first words are, "You should have been here an hour and five minutes ago." This remark produces in the audience a "general growl," after which K. announces in ringing tones his passionate devotion to the principle: "Whether I am late or not, I am here now." He fails to appreciate that he has no relevance once he is late; that the act of arrival is only a simulation of real arrival, its form rather than its substance; that he is not there and that he is not wanted, if indeed he ever was. We are dealing, on the whole, with multiple levels of inverted experience.

[2] For examples, see *The Married Couple* and *An Everyday Confusion*, as well, of course, as *The Great Wall of China*.

I O.

The Problem of Guilt

We have considered the proposal that Joseph K. may be an abstraction, not a person in the usual literary sense of the word, and have seen that if this is so, it has an important bearing upon the reasonableness of concluding that *The Trial* is allegory, as well as a significant effect upon the structure and organization of the material itself. The possible nature of the abstraction, however, deserves some attention, and the hypothesis is tenable that Joseph K. is an abstraction of guilt; that is, that Joseph K. is not guilty, but is guilt itself.

Guilt may in fact be the crime of which Joseph K. is accused, which would suggest that everything he does after the accusation and the arrest must itself be evidence of guilt, the actions, in short, of the guilty man. He thus brings about, inevitably, and because of what he is, his own destruction. He pursues his end with as much *implicit* purpose as Oedipus, in trying to discover the murderer of Laius, *explicitly* pursues his. It is perhaps this element in his behavior which Michel Carrouges had in mind when he called it "fatal comportement." In discussing the implacable nature of the Court in *The Trial*, Carrouges says:

Car la loi juridique ne cessera pas de [le] persécuter jusqu'à la mort, sans autre motif que le fatal comportement de Kafka lui-même.[3]

---

[3] *Kafka contre Kafka*, Paris: Plon, 1962, p. 63. Carrouges, for reasons which have to do with his own thesis, that *The Trial* is "le procès du fils par le père, du père par le fils et même du fils par le fils," identifies K. with Kafka without even momentary hesitation or doubt.

Perhaps in virtue of having been born, Joseph K. *s'est mis le doigt dans l'engrenage.*

Guilt, in its traditional form, has two aspects: the "reality" of guilt and the "feeling" of guilt. The concept of the nature of man as fallen, that every descendant of Adam has inherited a terrible bequest of suffering, that the human race is in consequence bound together by a solidarity of guilt, is built upon the "reality" of two things: the original act and the sinfulness of the original act. There is, in other words, a "real" guilt, inherent in the human condition, which is that of guilt, and each individual relates to this "real" guilt in the referential way of the Platonic universe: each individual is a particular guilty reflection of this ideal. The "feeling" of guilt may be that reaction to the condition which persists even when the "reality" of the guilt has been lost, a feeling which has lost sight of its ultimate cause:

> . . . guilt is a reality . . . we *feel* guilty because we *are* guilty, *but that feeling has been misplaced, dislocated from its true cause,* and is seeking some cause to which to attach itself.[4]

This cause may of course be ascribed to anterior injustice, to flaws in the system, to the misapplication of the system, to its corruption. The accusation of guilt may be considered to be false and quite possibly malicious, and this in turn can lead to the systematic pursuit of a defense. The futility of such a reaction, and the futility of the means Joseph K. employs as a result, is clear if the premiss that we *are* guilty is seen as having been converted by Kafka to the abstraction of guilt itself. For a feeling is different from the thing felt in that it is "like" it but it is not the same. None the less the essence may be derived from the feeling, which is its symptom, and

[4] Caryll Houselander, *Guilt*, New York: Sheed & Ward, 1951, p. 13. The italics are the author's.

we can sometimes thus determine what we are from what we are like. The difficulty is that the abstraction K. is not like anything; it is something *per se*, and K. himself, within the novel, is prevented from discovering who he is in part because he cannot have, and in fact does not have, any concern with what he is like, and cannot know, or hope to learn, anything of his nature. This is one of the inherent sources of the egoism which characterizes K., an egoism which has the superficial effect of making him disdainful of others, but the important one of alienating him from everybody else because, not being able to share the guilt of their common condition, he conceives himself as an isolated victim of a malicious plot. He lacks the empathy without which, within this reading of his abstraction, he cannot achieve his goal, that of entering the world from which he finds himself rejected and exiled. If we extrapolate this condition into that of love, K. is loveless because he cannot love, and he cannot love because he loves only himself. He not only fails to have an awareness of himself and a knowledge of who he is, but he gives evidence of wishing to evade it: in order to protect himself from a confrontation with his real sinfulness, he concerns himself exclusively with the constant examination and re-examination of his imagined sins, with the well-understood aim of trying in this way to secure relief from his suffering. That this can be suitably seen in terms of the figure of the doctrine of original sin, especially in its orthodox Catholic form, does not however suggest that this is what *The Trial* is all about. Joseph K. within *The Trial*, for reasons which have already been offered, is not an allegorical figure and not a symbol: the process with which the novel progresses makes it incompetent as either example or as vehicle for a view. If it were not, there would be no reason at all for a reader to whom, for example, the Catholic answer to the dilemma of man was an article of faith, not to see Joseph K. as a literary instance of a condition so common in the world,

77

especially since the Reformation, of man foolishly, stubbornly, and ignorantly refusing to surrender himself to the illimitable love of Christ. Such a solution would falsify the novel not because it is false in itself, but because the fabric of the novel's experience does not permit of any solution at all. Despite this, critical constructs and implied solutions which in their nature must be mutually exclusive, continue not only to thrive, but to live fairly comfortably next to each other. K. "fails to understand," as the critic may be, the Catholic world, the Protestant world, the orthodox Jewish world, the Reformed Jewish world, the nature of bourgeois society, the requirements for a contented proletariat, the love of father for son or of son for father. But his guilt in the novel is guilt *per se*, abstracted from guilt as a reflection of ideal guilt, for this is the only guilt possible in his world, despite the fact that he deduces from the vestigial stirrings within him of the feelings of guilt that now, as in the past, these feelings must be intimations of something else, of something "real." His reaction to these feelings may be compared to the reaction of a man whose leg has been amputated, to "sensations" he "feels" in the missing member. The stable world of values has changed, and the leg is gone, but "the melody," as the popular jazz song has it, "lingers on."

For what if there is in fact no real guilt, but only actions which we denominate as guilty? The question becomes clearer with the hypothesis that Joseph K., despite appearances to the contrary, may be inhabiting an existential universe, characterized in the main by the absence within it of *a priori* values, and consequently by the circumstance that values inhere in acts and in how we name acts. Every action, therefore, has a human subjectivity, as Sartre claims, and takes on whatever connotation it may bear only when it is deliberately given that connotation. It relates only to itself, not to any "real" value system, not to any external hierarchies. Guiltiness is an example of that sort of relative attribute—it comes into being not when a given act has been committed but when, after the commission, somebody calls it "guilty." It is, in other words, guiltiness only so long as it is recognized as such, and this would suggest that it can be abolished by an act of non-recognition, by a refusal to affirm it. If this is the nature of the world, and it is not necessary to think so to follow the argument, then the nature of self-awareness changes, and the knowledge of oneself that one needs changes in kind and character. It is no longer a question of deducing "real" guilt from feelings of guilt, and of recognizing that it cannot be avoided by avoiding suffering, but only by submission to Christ's boundless and uncompromising love. It is a matter of learning that guilt, existing only to the extent that we say it does, and to the exact, congruent degree, is within our power to control. We can wave the wand of our affirmation and cause it to spring up full-blown, or we can command it, like Aladdin's djinn, to return to its bottle and be forever corked. In the one case, self-knowledge consists of acceptance and an acknowledgment of weakness; in the other, self-knowledge consists of strength and an estimate of power. In the one case reason does not work—on the contrary, it interferes, holds one, in Donne's terms, "in thrall," and makes one yearn to have one's heart battered; in the other case acceptance does not work, because there is nothing to accept. The irony in *The Trial* lies in the fact that it gives the appearance of representing the futility of reason and hence of suggesting the validity of acceptance: we tend to ascribe Joseph K.'s failure in part to his insistence upon evaluating his circumstances rationally when they are not. This would seem to be the burden of the priest's remarks in the cathedral, and the import of the total scene of the first interrogation, and is also suggested by Frau Grubach when she comments about K.'s arrest: "It gives me the feeling of something very learned, forgive me if what I say is stupid, it gives me the feeling of something abstract which I don't understand but which I don't need to understand either."

Furthermore, from the relatively low position Frau Grubach occupies on the social scale, we can assume that a certain amount of weight deserves to be given to her reactions.[5]

The futility may, however, stem not from Joseph K.'s use of reason in an irrational world, but from his misuse of reason in a rational one, reason which has lost its power to be effective not because reason as such cannot be effective, but because its particular forms and referents are no longer relevant. For the language of reason, the language of the syllogism, is symbol (which requires an external reality) and order (which requires integrity and stability); it is based upon, and reflects, a world which is "orderly" in the sense that logic is "orderly." But logic may be orderly, and conclusions reasonable, without having any reference at all to what exists, for syllogisms are only "true" by virtue of the relationship of their terms, not by virtue of their applicability to anything outside themselves. The formal language which K. uses, the linguistic figure of the novel, is perhaps only the shell of reason; it cannot, as a matter of fact, be other in an existential world. Paralysis thus ensues, for no action can be taken which is effective. There is a hint of this, and a hint that for a fleeting moment Joseph K. may have a glimpse of the knowledge which, within the novel's postulates, he must have if he is to act at all, and that is at a point in the first interrogation. K., emboldened by his estimate that one of the divisions of the spectators is of some consequence, says:

[5] It is not by accident that a large proportion of the persons through whom God has chosen in the past to speak have been of lowly origin, of limited education, or both. Joan of Arc is perhaps the best known example, but there are others, including a farm wife in a remote section of Minnesota whose wrists and ankles started spontaneously to bleed, from no apparent cause, somewhere around 1941. Nor is it unusual that the Angel Moroni, when he wished to make his holy tablets, written in a strange tongue, available to the public, should have entrusted them to Joseph Smith, who had had no linguistic training, nor that he should have chosen to reveal them to Smith in a small backyard in upstate New York.

The Problem of Guilt

This question of yours, Herr Examining Magistrate, about
my being a house-painter—or rather, not a question, you
simply made a statement—is typical of the whole character
of this trial that is being foisted on me. You may object
that it is not a trial at all; you are quite right, for it is
only a trial if I recognize it as such.

If it is only a trial to the extent that K. recognizes it as such,
it will no longer be a trial when and if K. ceases to recognize it,
and he thus has it within his power to disaffirm it, and, by
disaffirming it, to free himself from it. Reason, (empirical and
relevant analysis of the actual) might tell him this, and comes
very close indeed to doing so; the *form* of reason (discourse on
indicative and subjunctive levels, with logical alternatives and
classifications) must fail. By the same token, what applies
in this passage to the trial may also apply to K.'s condition
of guilt: he is guilty only so long as he chooses to consider
himself guilty. Since he never fails to consider himself guilty,
he must be arraigned and punished for being guilty, and he is,
no less for saying, with Terence, *"si peccavi, insciens feci."* It
is in the sense, then, that K. is abstract guilt and its condition
rather than their sign or symbol, that we should consider the
relevance of original sin, as a figure rather than as a subject.
As Georges Henein puts it, in discussing *The Trial*,

> . . . on a le droit de se demander si Kafka n'a pas voulu
> remettre en scène . . . la farce la plus cruelle que l'humanité
> ait eu à subir: l'histoire du péché originel.[6]

The essence of this comment lies in the words "remettre en
scène," the stage serving as analogue of the movements of
Kafka's abstract marionettes who dance out the pattern of sin,
not sin itself.

[6] In *Clé*, No. 2, 1939. Used by Carrouges, *op. cit.*, as one of a list of
opinions about Kafka which he appends to his book. There is a
suspicion that Henein thinks that *The Trial* is *about* original sin, or
else Carrouges, who has a strong *parti pris*, probably would not have
referred to him.

The Process of Kafka's *Trial*

If we assume that K.'s guiltiness has no greater extent than his willingness to think of himself as guilty, and that he could cause it to disappear by disaffirming it, we see that he has a power which is useless to him because he does not know that he has it. That this power, once noticed and used, could free man in the substantive meaning of the word, may be well understood by those who depend upon keeping man enslaved and caught up in the toils of a system. The authorities, who would lose all if man were once to affirm his right and his ability to live without any papers, have a vested interest in seeing to it that the value of those papers should always be accepted. Zeus, in Sartre's play *The Flies*, is well aware of how precarious the position of the gods is. In Act I he takes occasion to remind an old woman of the importance of earning forgiveness through repentance. The old woman, shaking with fear, replies:

> Oh, sir, I do repent, most heartily I repent. If you only knew how I repent, and my daughter, too, and my son-in-law offers up a heifer every year, and my little grandson has been brought up in a spirit of repentance. He is a pretty lad, with flaxen hair, and he always behaves as good as gold. Though he's only seven, he never plays or laughs, for thinking of his original sin.

To which Zeus, eminently satisfied, answers:

> Good, you old bitch, that's as it should be—and be sure you die in a nice bitchy odor of repentance. It's your one hope of salvation.[7]

Of Joseph K. we might say, with Zeus, after the old woman scuttles away: "Unless I'm much mistaken, my masters, we have there *the real thing*, the good old piety of yore, rooted in terror."[8]

[7] Jean-Paul Sartre, *The Flies*, trans. Stuart Gilbert. New York: Vintage Books (V-16) n.d., pp. 56–57.
[8] *Ibid.* Italics added.

II.

Literary Structure in an Existential Universe

One of the consequences of a universe in which actions relate only to themselves, and have no significance apart from that which may be given to them from time to time within a human subjectivity, is that the literary vehicles of these actions, characters, can be nothing but themselves, a point already made with respect to Joseph K. But if the characters and their actions are nothing but themselves, it follows that the material of the novel must be composed entirely of itself as well: whatever the point of view from which the experiences are perceived, there can be no other, and nothing else can be seen. There is evidence to suggest that Stephen Crane, as long ago as 1895, fell for one reason or another into this conclusion, for in *The Red Badge of Courage* we have one of the earliest examples of this phenomenon, that nothing occurs which is not within the vision of the single pair of eyes possessed by the protagonist, Henry Fleming. The novel is therefore not only composed of its own materials, but as a result it cannot have any normative materials against which to compare or contrast it. Again, in the case of Michel Butor's *La Modification*, it is only in the course of time that we become aware of the fact that while it does not ever appear as such, there is an implied consciousness behind the "action," behind the progress of the "modification" which takes place. It is character through implication only, just as the jealousy which would appear to be a central theme in Alain Robbe-Grillet's *La Jalousie* is not jealousy in the ordinary meaning of the term, but the total of the interpretations of events, seen narrowly through the slats of *"une jalousie,"* of a man who exists only inferentially.

The inferential man cannot "stand" for anything nor can he ever "see" anything which is not there. Among the things which he cannot see are the absurdities of the world, the irrelevancies of the world and, of course, the significant values of the world. For the world

> . . . is neither significant nor absurd. It *is*, quite simply. That, in any case, is the most remarkable thing about it. And suddenly the obviousness of this strikes us with irresistible force. All at once the whole splendid construction collapses; opening our eyes unexpectedly, we have experienced, once too often, the shock of this stubborn reality we were pretending to have mastered. Around us, defying the noisy pack of our animistic or protective adjectives, things *are there. . . .*[9]

What has happened as a result of the *presence* of things must have consequences with respect to the nature and function of the characters. They may

> . . . suggest many possible interpretations; they may, according to the preoccupations of each reader, accommodate all kinds of comment—psychological, psychiatric, religious, or political—yet their indifference to these 'potentialities' will soon be apparent. Whereas the traditional hero is constantly solicited, caught up, destroyed by these interpretations of the author's, ceaselessly projected into an immaterial and unstable *elsewhere*, always more remote and blurred, the future hero will remain, on the contrary, *there*. It is the commentaries that will be left elsewhere; in the face of his irrefutable presence, they will seem useless, superfluous, even improper.[10]

Robbe-Grillet says, in 1956, that this will be the nature of the future hero. It is, in fact, the nature of Kafka's hero, Joseph K., thirty-one years before.

[9] Alain Robbe-Grillet, "A Future for the Novel," in *For a New Novel*, New York: Grove Press, 1965, p. 19. The essay was originally written in 1956.

[10] Alain Robbe-Grillet, *op. cit.*, p. 22.

Literary Structure in an Existential Universe

It is the "presence" of things which leads to the techniques of the "*nouveau-roman*," among them the substitution of the sensitive film for the analytical eye. It is the same "presence" of things which leads Kafka to the use of static images, but there is an important difference. The "*nouveau-roman*" has its own sense of movement, the movement of the cinema, which is made up of the *rapid* succession of individual frames. In Kafka, the individual frames succeed each other deliberately and slowly, one after the other, but with perceptible pauses. It is the difference between the showing of slides and the showing of a movie. In Kafka, consequently, a paralysis of time results, whereas in the "*nouveau-roman*" time is not so much paralyzed as slowed down, speeded up, or compressed. Michel Butor's novel, *l'Emploi du Temps*,[11] is an excellent example of these uses of time. As the novel progresses from page to page, the chronological gap between the dates of the diary entries and the events which they record becomes narrower, until at the end we are in the "present" of both event and recording of event.

This is not, however, a matter of technique alone, although from analysis of the technique the circumstances giving rise to it may be adduced. Often a technical structure is misread because we forget that in addition to structure, there must be taken into account the attitude towards the nature of the universe which underlies it, and no structure will in itself necessarily convey existential experience, although some structures are particularly well fitted to do so. A case in point is Faulkner's *The Sound and the Fury*, in which it requires a certain amount of time before the reader becomes aware of the fact that he is looking at the world from within the unique and special experience of a congenital idiot, Benjy. The implication of the consciousness behind the statements of Benjy

[11] Paris: Editions de Minuit, 1957.

85

comes to us in the *same manner* as the implication of the consciousness behind the protagonists of *La Jalousie* or of *La Modification*, but with a significant difference. In the case of *The Sound and the Fury* we interpret, and hence "understand" this consciousness as *representative* initially of the condition of feeblemindedness and, later, of the state of innocence or purity which becomes, within the novel, the norm by which the more traditionally presented viewpoints of Jason and Quentin are judged. Benjy's muteness is thus a sign of the muteness of Christ, of the "word swaddled in darkness," and regardless of what we make of this in particular, we can be assured in general that Faulkner's universe is one of *a priori* values, and that his writing functions in traditional ways. We have, in other words, normative matter lying outside the material of the novel; it only appears at first that we do not. In the novels of Robbe-Grillet and Butor, however, when the consciousness is implied it is only *there*. We know nothing about it apart from what it is conscious of, nor is there anything in the novels other than what the consciousness is conscious of. As a consequence, we cannot, for example, judge whether the consciousness is conscious of "all there is," or only partially aware; we cannot state that the consciousness is an "infantile" one, or a "mature" one, or a "normative" one. While we do not have to be content that Benjy's viewpoint in *The Sound and the Fury* is the only viewpoint, we must be content that the viewpoints in *La Jalousie* and *La Modification* are. We can thus use Benjy's viewpoint to judge others, while there can be no judgment in *La Jalousie* or *La Modification*. It is never "right," or "wrong," or "desirable," or "regrettable" that when the protagonist of *La Modification* arrives in Rome, he does not do what he may have had it in mind to do when he boarded the train in Paris. It is, however, regrettable that for reasons of his mutilation and his retardation, Benjy can never hope to be heard.

For no technique in literature can by itself produce a revolution of the attitude of the author. He will not succeed in producing a reflection of the existential world by his pen alone, any more than Flaubert could, by his assiduous attention to the techniques of realism, exorcise from *Madame Bovary* his fundamentally romantic view of the world. Such an attempt is futile, and futile in the same way, and for the same reasons, as Joseph K.'s attempts to orient himself in an existential world through the application of techniques from the *a priori* world from which he is alienated because it no longer exists.

I 2 .

The Inversion of Crime and Punishment

The possibility that Joseph K. may be an abstraction of guilt, rather than a symbol for guilt, carries with it yet another implication, that the usual sequence of punishment coming after the crime has been reversed by Kafka. When a character is a condition of guilt, every act which he subsequently commits is by that token a guilty act, and if we consider his state of guilt to be in the nature of punishment, it comes before the crime, not after. As a result, the guilty man is driven to discovering his crime, and it is in this frenzied search for the crime, brought about by his punishment, that he actually commits it. The problem may perhaps be seen in terms of familiar social phenomena: the state of coming from a degraded, or a psychologically disoriented environment, insofar as it sets such a person apart from those who do not, may be thought of as a punishment. The child of genetically unsound parents, to the extent that he has inherited their unstable or retarded characteristics, is being punished for being who he is: it is certainly not a consequence of a criminal act as

87

such. In the same way, the youngster who must grow up in extreme poverty, to the degree that this experience is different from the experience of more fortunate children, is being punished for being who he is, in this case the child of extremely poor parents. This punishment, however, may in turn lead to the commission of "crimes," and hence come after, not before them. In turn, society in general, and its victims in particular, accept this judgment and conclude that since punishment is being inflicted, it must be deserved; and if the precise nature of the crime which has brought about the punishment is not immediately discernible, it must be found. It is the business, in other words, of the Furies to come before the act, not after, and to drive the individual to his crime. For otherwise, the crime, having no owner, will start to prowl "round the city, whimpering like a dog that has lost its master."[12] The poor thus often accept the fact that they are suffering because they are poor, and are poor because they deserve to be. As another case in point, one of the greatest problems facing, in 1966, the civil rights movement in America, has been that of convincing Negroes that blackness is no crime and that they should no longer accept the judgment of the white world that their unhappy lot is itself a sign of their inferiority, and hence deserved. Thus Joseph K. is never free from the conclusion that he would not have been arrested if he had not been guilty of something, and he is so obsessed with the obligation to chase his crime that he seeks out the Court on his own volition, even though he has been released by the officials who arrested him in the first place. The warders originally suggest that the legal officials never hunt for crime themselves but are, rather, drawn towards the guilty. This is how the situation appears to ignorant civil servants who know only the superficial aspects of the system which they serve. They have, after all, no reason to find such a view incorrect, as in their own experience they have never arrested anybody

[12] Jean-Paul Sartre, *op. cit.*, p. 126.

who was not guilty, since it is a sign of guilt to be arrested in the first place. But their understanding is limited and, in this instance, quite erroneous, for the truth may well be that the guilty are drawn to the law in an effort to discover their crime. Certainly the manner in which K. reaches the chambers of the first interrogation would seem to be evidence of this: he himself decides, in the face of its manifest absurdity, that he will go there on a Sunday; he makes an extraordinary effort to find the exact location of the rooms, enquires here and there, overcomes the evidence of his senses that he cannot possibly be in a neighborhood where it is likely that a Court would sit; pushes his way into the hearing against a number of obstacles, and arrives to confront the Examining Magistrate quite exhausted from his own labors to get there. Only a very powerful attraction could account for such behavior. Force has certainly not been applied to K. by the law, but K. has none the less sought the law out. He is like the figure of the guilty man suggested by Clytemnestra in Act I of Sartre's *The Flies*, when she talks to Electra about the nature of sin:

> But wait, my girl; one day you too, will be trailing after you an inexpiable crime. At every step you will think that you are leaving it behind, but it will remain as heavy as before. Whenever you look back you will see it there, just at arm's length, glowing darkly like a black crystal . . . and nothing remains for you but to drag your crime after you until you die.[13]

In this fashion the denial of guilt is transformed into the most obvious and the most heinous crime of all, and all of the defensive devices by which it is effected can only have the result of defeating themselves. The Examining Magistrate is well aware of this at the close of the first interrogation when he tells K. that he has "flung away [with his own hand] all the advantages which an interrogation invariably confers on an accused man."

[13] *Op. cit.*, p. 72.

13.

The Inversion of Sex and Wooing

This inversion of crime and punishment is one of a series of inversions in which *The Trial* abounds, and is corollary to them. The element of inversion is carried by reversals of ordinary sequences, foreshadowed and subsumed in the initial act of the arrest of Joseph K. We have seen some of them, the "process" of the law, the inversion of time, the backward movement as opposed to arrival, and the inversion of the traditional religious experience. Another example is to be found in the inversion of the customary sexual experience, which ordinarily is preceded by a series of introductory dalliances, constituting in that way the culmination of an intimacy which presumably has had to grow through progressive stages. Indeed it is not merely fortuitous that orgasm is referred to as "climax," which implies its culminatory element as well as all that must have preceded it; as "climax" it can also serve as goal and thus invest the totality of the sexual act with an immanent sense of progress, and hence of meaning.[14] But in Kafka's world in general,

[14] This inherent teleology of the sexual act has been so thoroughly appreciated by the contemporary generation that a great deal of primary attention has become focussed on the techniques by which it might be achieved, giving currency to suitable manuals of methodology. Indeed, it is understood that no happiness is possible between a man and a woman unless a satisfactory, and mutual, orgasm has been reached by both, simultaneously. Since it is recognized that this is often not possible without due care to the nature of the proceedings, an assiduous attention to the elements in sexual relationships which precede the climax is encouraged, and for that reason the sexual partners have a reinforcement of the feeling that they are participating in meaningful process and hence in a reasonable world. This may be a device to keep at bay the gulf of relativism of the sort which yawns before K.

and in *The Trial* in particular, the climactic sexual act occurs
before the relationships which customarily precede it. It is only
post coitum that the partners make any effort to meet, or to
know each other. In this fashion Leni deduces that K. "belongs
to her now" when K. falls down on the carpet with her as a
result of trying to keep her from falling off his lap. What
happens after the sexual act becomes in this order of events
a justification for the act—the consequences have come first,
not second. The chapter "Fräulein Bürstner's Friend" can be
understood in this light, for at its end K. is left in the position
of a disappointed suitor, or lover, who has not, however, evei
had any relationship at all with the object of his desires; the
disappointment comes before the rejection and postulates the
rejection as the punishment postulates the crime. In this case
K. will have to pursue Fräulein Bürstner, if he should ever
have the time to do so, in order to reach the antecedent of
the state in which he finds himself. But the fact that he has
the feeling of rejection, disappointment, and frustration is proof
enough to him that there must be a reason for them and that
consequently Fräulein Bürstner has turned him down. He thus
goes through a number of steps appropriate to a lover who
has been turned down and who wants to find out, if he can,
why, perhaps suspecting that there is another man involved
to whom his suit has lost. K. cautiously opens Fräulein Bürstner's door, and then is shocked when he sees Fräulein Bürstner and the Captain talking together, in low voices and with
an abstracted air which excludes him. Like all men who have
discovered the "truth" of their disappointment in love, K. feels

---

and may thus be an example of sexual reactionaryism in the face of
the encroachment of existential intimations. The man who fails to
bring about mutual orgasm, incidentally, feels "guilty" and may try
to "atone" by chasing down his "crime" in handbooks of sexual techniques or by consulting a priest/physician. In any case, this does not
affect the argument with respect to K.

small and heavy, the glances of the pair "weighed heavily" upon him, and he retires in anguish to his room to lick his wounds. But in fact K. has never had any relationship at all with Fräulein Bürstner. The sequence of events has been turned around.

K. is thus guilty of being rejected and since he is, the rejection is "deserved." The sexual connection is a means of making contact with the world, since it has within it an essential element of gratuity and is dual in its nature, for like the proverbial tango, it requires two, and two is always more than one and always involves an "other." But the condition of guilt of which K. is the literary abstraction is that of being rejected, and he does not "deserve" to re-enter the world because if he did, he would not have been initially expelled from it. He therefore does not, and cannot, "deserve" to have a successful sexual relationship, which must be defined as one in which the act of intercourse is the culmination, and indeed the final expression, of all the precedent processes and thus able to serve as means of contact with the world. All that remains, therefore, of this act of contact is the *form* of the act, the physical penetration in itself, and for that reason this *form* occurs *first*, so that if it has any sequelae, they relate to what should have come first and are not sequelae at all. As an act devoid of any sequential rationale, the sexual act can therefore occur in irrelevant circumstances, and does. Moreover, this casual aspect of sex in Kafka's works should not be interpreted as a sign of a casual attitude towards sex of either Kafka himself, or of his characters, nor as a symbol of their psychological incapacity to love, nor of their infantile retrogressions into primary sensations. The fact is that this *is* the nature of sex under the conditions of the nature of the Kafkan universe; any other sexual relationship would falsify the experience. The sexual act devoid of antecedent, and hence devoid of any goal other than itself, denies the duality which is implicit in sexual relationships, and since this duality is a function of the operation within the sexual context of two *distinct* individuals whose apartness is affirmed by the act, the purely *formal* act converts one of the individuals from person to object, and to object which does not have any particular, individual, unique qualities. At the least, from the duality of male and female, however, this one sexual difference can be understood as remaining, because even the conversion to object cannot get rid of it entirely. It is for this reason that we often react to the activities of a busy prostitute, or to those of a woman who is raped or entered by a constant succession of men, with feelings that we are in the presence of a form of brutality, wherein we recognize that there remains nothing of the woman under such circumstances apart from her female-ness, or suitability as object of a certain use. Nor does this use have to be entirely sexual. K., for example, remarks to the priest in Chapter IX, "In the Cathedral": "Women have great influence. If I could move some women I know to join forces in working for me, I couldn't help winning through. Especially before this Court, which consists almost entirely of petticoat-hunters." He would seem to be echoing Juvenal: *"Nulla fere causa est in qua non femina litem moverit."*[15]

Now for an "object" we can have that sentiment which we call "pity"; indeed, we have pity only when we see the recipient of our pity *as* object. Pity does not imply empathy, but on the contrary, is a function of distance, and it does not carry with it any implied statements concerning the right of the pitied to that pity. There is thus between him who pities and him who is pitied a great gap: the one who pities is in a world which the pitied person *can never hope to enter;* if, as a matter of fact, he could, he would sacrifice his possibility of being pitied. We can therefore pity conditions, provided they are neither our own nor close to our own in space or

[15] *Satires*, VI, 242.

time, for our pity increases as the gap is wider. Between Joseph K. and the world which he wishes to enter, or to enter again, there is so wide a gap that the only connection he can have with it at all is that of pity, and since the act which constitutes the most significant act of connection is the act of sex, the act of sex becomes an act of pity, and nothing more. And this is emphasized by the circumstances that the women in *The Trial* and *The Castle* with whom K. has sexual relationships are themselves of the lowest order in the substantive world—they are servants, barmaids, assistants, hangers-on— with whom under normal conditions K.'s social snobbery would make it out of the question to have any relations at all. They may even be deformed: Leni has webbing between her fingers, and it is this deformed hand which K. uncontrollably kisses, calling it a "pretty little paw" and a "freak of nature." But low though they may be in social rank, and deformed though they may be in physical appearance, the one fundamental advantage they have over K. which makes them capable of offering pity, not receiving it, is that they are in the world, and K. is not; and there is between K. and even the lowest section of that world an unbridgeable, permanent, intractable gap. From Fräulein Bürstner, on the other hand, a woman of K.'s own position in society, a woman with whom in theory a dual and satisfactory relationship is conceivable, K. cannot even elicit pity. Her fleeting appearance as K. goes towards his execution is illusory and evanescent and does not satisfy even that requirement. The only possible relationship with Fräulein Bürstner is that second-hand and syllogistic one which he has not with her, but about her, in his interminable conversation with Fräulein Montag, a conversation which must surely be the most perfect example of utter frustration and of the complete breakdown of effective human contact.

1 4 .

The Paradigm of Desuetude

This breakdown of effective contact, which confronts the reader, and Joseph K., throughout *The Trial*, is conveyed through two devices which complement each other. The first is the choice, as subject matter for elaborate and logical discussion, of an element which is ancillary or irrelevant to the substance, so that even if the discussion were able to arrive at some enlightening conclusion, it would have served to enlighten only a point which is of no importance in any case. The second is the obsessive use of the *form* of language which presupposes not only a logical universe of referents, but the possibility of achieving rational order through the inclusion of every alternative within a constantly growing series of syllogistic propositions. We have seen that the nearest "objective correlative" of this linguistic form is the language of the law. Indeed, it is this characteristic which sets the language of the law sufficiently apart from ordinary language to make it recognizable as a special idiom, a recognition from which it draws a certain added verisimilitude. The breakdown of contact, with its consequent collapse into desuetude, stems thus from the inherent innocuity of the method. But this innocuity is doubled, so to speak, when it is devoted in the first place to the clarification of a situation which itself is entirely irrelevant; the ineffectiveness is thus increased, and the action is inconsequential at an additional remove. The contrast between the fervor, and often the brilliance, of the effort, and the failure to achieve any significant result, is so great that it carries with it its own concomitant of despair, in which there is no longer even failure in the accepted connotation of the

95

word, but rather a gigantic fizzle in which everything peters out in a bootless sputter, "not with a bang, but a whimper." The structure, then, of the novel's argument is in itself the structure of fizzle, and the process of the argument is an extended, indeed omnipresent, figure, of the irrelevance of the traditional processes of thought and of the nature of the process/trial through which Joseph K. analogously moves. It has thus a dialectic pattern which bears the weight of the overall figure itself, and is integral to the essence of futility of which it is both cause and victim.

One of the clearest, and earliest, examples of this is to be found in the first chapter, "The Arrest," at a point where K. and the Inspector are discussing the morning's events. "You are," says the Inspector at one stage of the conversation, "presumably very surprised at the events of this morning?" There are three points of reference within this question: the events themselves and the difficult circumstances of the arrest, the unexpectedness to K. of these events and his consequent surprise at them, and the degree of this surprise. In order of relevancy, and hence of substantive importance, they may be considered in that order, the last being not only relatively unimportant but of no effective relationship to the critically important first element. It is this last element, however, which K. chooses to make the subject of his concern: "Certainly," he responds, "I am surprised, but I am by no means very surprised." The Inspector is surprised by this response and says "Not very surprised?", opening up a field of discussion which suggests that K. should explain why he is only surprised and not very surprised. Of course the question of his being surprised at all is irrelevant, and the conversation must now proceed at least two levels away from the issue of the arrest which it is apparently engaged in clarifying. K. is quick to appreciate that in stating that he was only surprised, and not very surprised, he has apparently confessed to a reaction which the Inspector thinks is improper, and may therefore have placed himself at a further disadvantage. He is certainly guilty, in his own mind, of having not been very surprised, and immediately recants: "I mean that I am very surprised, of course . . ." Now he realizes that he must clarify what appears to be a contradiction between his first response and his second; he cannot now admit to being very surprised without denying his original statement that he was only surprised, and he proceeds to do so by suggesting that a man of his years may be expected to have become accustomed to a certain number of surprises so that after a time his capacity to be surprised normally will have been diminished. At this point, he offers an example of the origin of common surprises in the world of the experienced man, and of the frequent occurrence of jokes. He is not, however, ready to say that the circumstances of his arrest are the result of a joke: "I won't say that I regard the whole thing as a joke. . . ," and then offers a series of reasons why it is not possible for him to state without equivocation that it is in fact a joke. Among these reasons are the fact that "the whole staff of the boarding-house would have to be involved, as well as all you people, and that would be past a joke." To which the Inspector assents. "So," concludes K., "I don't say that it is a joke." At the same time, K. has reason to think that it may well be a joke. For one thing, a joke is not an affair of importance, and K. finds some elements in his situation which suggest that he is involved in a purely minor matter: "I argue this from the fact that though I am accused of something, I cannot recall the slightest offence that might be charged against me." The only conclusion from all of this can be that K. has good and sufficient reason not to have been very surprised. Such elaboration of close reasoning can lead no further, first because it is directed at a non-essential element, second because in any case there is reason to think that the world which has been disclosed to K. by the act of arrest is not amenable to manipulation by the tools of a dead era.

In the chapter "Fräulein Bürstner's Friend" this figure is repeated, with more devastating failure if we consider that in soliciting the attention of Fräulein Bürstner, K. may well be making the only move he ever does make in the novel (or later in *The Castle*) towards a meaningful contact with another human being. There is the faintest suggestion that what K. feels towards Fräulein Bürstner is the closest he ever gets to a feeling of love. It is not certain that this is what he feels, but it is certainly not so thoroughly excluded as a possibility as it is in all the other contacts he has with women, such as the liaison with Leni and his relationship, in *The Castle*, with Frieda. Not only are these other relationships affected by the inversion of sex and wooing to which we have already alluded, but they are in addition characterized by the circumstance that in each case K. hopes to be able to derive some particular advantage to his cause from the women: for example, he hopes to gain something from Frieda's closeness to Klamm. The women are thus not only converted by the nature of sex without antecedent into objects, they are also converted into objects of further utility, and it may be presumed that if and when they are unable to be useful they will lose whatever value to K. they may have had. There is, however, no evidence, in K.'s yearning for Fräulein Bürstner, of any more self-interest than that which normally inheres in any act of loving—love solicits love, but this is the extent of its serving of self. At any rate, K. merely would like to have an opportunity to talk with Fräulein Bürstner, to explain his conduct, to have, not some sort of tumultuous affair, but no more than an interview. The importunate suitor is not an unfamiliar figure, and he must expect to be accepted or rejected. If he is rejected he may have gloomy thoughts, but he can ascribe his gloom to having been rejected; his wounds have an origin which, if it does not allay the pain, at least explains them and places them into a manageable frame of reference. The disappointed suitor is the opposite of the successful suitor; each implies the other, and thus the state of being either is to that extent supportable. In K.'s situation with respect to Fräulein Bürstner, though, his suit is not even a suit, but a request for the possible preliminary to a suit. He wants a personal interview, and to his requests for one there has been no answer at all from Fräulein Bürstner. Ultimately, however, he receives a message from a friend of Fräulein Bürstner's, Fräulein Montag, that she would like to speak to him on behalf of Fräulein Bürstner, not in Fräulein Bürstner's room, to which he would like to be admitted, but in another room so filled with a dining table that there is almost no space for two people; it is "almost inaccessible," so that even this distant contact is available to K. only barely. K. in this circumstance is once more seen in the position of petitioner, this time to Fräulein Bürstner, who has the power to grant or not to grant an interview, and once more we see K. in the position of being removed by great distance from the object of his petition. As in the first interrogation, moreover, the power (Fräulein Bürstner) moves through underlings and deputies who know nothing of the entire system but only a small part which relates to their function within it. They know, as the warders know, however, that they would not have been called upon to function at all if there had not been good and sufficient reason. Fräulein Montag says, for example, that Fräulein Bürstner must know what the interview would have consisted of, and further know that it would have been useless, but she does not know the reasons, "of which I am ignorant." Fräulein Montag does not even continue to accept the formal position of a conversation, face to face across a table, but opens the discussion while she casually trails her handbag the whole length of the room. The linguistic paradigm is the same as in K.'s elaboration of the possibility that the arrest was

99

nothing but a joke: to K.'s remark that Fräulein Montag's
presence as surrogate for Fräulein Bürstner is evidence that
Fräulein Bürstner decided not to grant his petition for a personal interview, Fräulein Montag responds with a consideration
of the problem of what interviews in general are, since obviously if what K. had asked of Fräulein Bürstner were not
an interview, or if what he had asked, that an interview be
granted, were not possible because interviews are not susceptible
to being granted or not granted, it would be false to assume
from her presence that Fräulein Bürstner had made a decision
of the sort which K. concludes she must have made: "Surely,
in general," Fräulein Montag says in pursuit of this point,
"interviews are neither deliberately accepted nor refused. But
it may happen that one sees no point in an interview, and that
is the case here." The next step, of course, is to consider the
conditions under which interviews may become pointless, and
hence not permitted to occur. Fräulein Montag reports that
Fräulein Bürstner came to the conclusion that an interview
with K. would be pointless in part "because [he] could not
attach very much importance to the interview either, for it
could only have been by accident that [he] hit upon the
idea." Fräulein Montag is responsible for making this clear
to K.: she herself stands sponsor for the proposition that "the
slightest uncertainty even in the most trifling matter is always
a worry"; and her service as intermediary was her own idea.
As far as we can tell, Fräulein Bürstner was not only disin-
terested in the whole affair as a general thing, but she saw no
reason to make further explanations of her having failed to
respond to K., although she had no objection to such explanations being made by Fräulein Montag if Fräulein Montag
wished to do so. Nor is Fräulein Montag certain that what
she represents as Fräulein Bürstner's attitude is in fact her
attitude—she merely assumes that it is, so there is always a
possibility that even that clarification which she offers to K. is
erroneous. At any rate, at the conclusion of this logical exer-

cise, offered in the analogous framework of the language of formal rhetoric and the setting of formal communication, no communication whatsoever has taken place; indeed, K. leaves the interview with Fräulein Montag neither rejected nor not rejected, neither free nor not free, no closer than he ever was to his objective, in an ineffectual sputter which is not even the consequence of the dousing of a flame. The pattern of his attempt to reach Fräulein Bürstner is that of his attempt to reach the truth of the law, in language, in figure, and in result. The irrelevancy is not, as we might assume, a statement of irrelevancy, nor the consequence of a failure to find a relevant approach, which in turn would suggest, as K. himself thinks, some failure in himself properly or intelligently to act; rather, it is inherent in the structure of the scene and is an abstraction, so to speak, of irrelevancy itself, with which, as in a painting, we are in fact confronted in all its delineaments. It is not subject to change.

1 5 .

The Ambivalence of Exclusion

The heart of the matter is therefore the distance which separates the user of the manipulative tools from the object upon which he is trying to have an effect. The tools are in themselves unchanged in form, but they were created with attention to their applicability to objects which no longer exist. All that can possibly remain to the user is to wave them about as he used to do, but without managing to accomplish anything at all, not even a misuse. This would seem to be the significance of the legal rhetoric in which the novel is couched. It is a rhetoric which, when it related to an external reality, had its

own value and contained the possibility of effect, but it would
be a mistake to consider this only in these terms. Legal
rhetoric itself, however distinct it may be from the ordinary,
is none the less only a particularly exemplary form of a
system of argumentation on which the rational world of order
is based and from which, as a matter of fact, the rhetoric itself,
and its formal patterns, may be originally derived. It represents in general, as the specifically legal elements represent
in particular, the linguistic form which the struggle of man to
create order out of chaos reflects, and it consequently contains
within it a certain immanent optimism which suggests that
such an orderly creation, although perhaps not simple, is
conceivably within the grasp of man's powers. This immanent
optimism leads to the conclusion, when a particular effort has
failed to accomplish anything, that the failure is to be ascribed
to a misapplication of the method, to a flaw in the logical
chain, to an improper balance of the terms of the syllogism.
Such an anterior flaw is parallel to that anterior flaw which
Joseph K. suspects when he is faced with his arrest, and in
turn leads to some further conclusions: that there must be a
process involved and hence the situation is not, so to speak,
ad hoc; that the flaw can be repaired by going back to the
point of error, or, if it cannot be repaired, that it can be
regretted and ascribed to the fundamental flaw of the human
condition, which is another way of saying that as men, there
are steps which we cannot take and depths of understanding
which we cannot have. Thus Oedipus analyzes his situation,
when he first hears rumors to the effect that he is a bastard,
and acts upon the rational conclusions of his analysis: if it is
fated that he should kill his father and marry his mother, it
is wise to leave his father and his mother, since if he is
separated from them, neither of these two acts can come about.
He therefore sets out from Corinth and has, by that act, put
into practise what his reason teaches him, and manipulated

the universe as effectively as possible with the tools at his disposal. These tools, however, are faulty, not because Oedipus reasons incorrectly, but because the tools relate to the universe of man. The ironic fact that in leaving Corinth, Oedipus brings about what he was trying to avoid, is not a condemnation of the logic of his reason, but is a statement that reason has its limits, and that man cannot overcome the limits of his human condition. Indeed the ability of the reader to appreciate the irony inheres in his conviction that under the circumstances Oedipus has acted as sensibly as *any man could*. This context, essential to the idea of retribution, and critical to the idea of redemption, is only, however, one of the two alternatives open when it is presumed that a set of circumstances is ascribable to an anterior error. The other, of course, is that of Joseph K.— to try to go back to the point where the mistake was made— but whether or not the damage is reparable, both points of view share the assumption that there is process and that, in consequence, there is order. Tragedy would appear to be the literary result of the second alternative, but this makes it a variation in the attitude towards experience, not something outside the experience, and tragedy thus contains within it the ambiguity that while it seems to question the moral order of the universe and, indeed, in the form of the qualm, does in fact question it, it does not question it at all in a substantive manner but, on the contrary, reaffirms it more strongly than ever. Tragedy contains within it the twin reactions of rejection and acceptance: the power of the acceptance depends upon the power of the rejection which it has served to overcome, and hence its statement of the need to overcome rejection is made even the more clarion. This ambiguity of rejection and acceptance may be seen vestigially in Joseph K. himself. He is pulled on most occasions by contradictory forces. He wants to be "free," but at the same time his position with respect to the world, that of rejected man, gives him an overwhelmingly powerful desire to be accepted; that is, if he were by some miracle to be able to achieve his goal, this goal would involve being accepted and, hence, accepting, his place, his rôle, his identity. Joseph K. is far from being a revolutionary, but he displays that ambivalence towards the "establishment" which characterizes so many revolutionaries, who are motivated in part to destroy or modify the world because they have been unable to find a place in it (as Othello, perhaps, is moved to kill Desdemona), in the same manner that overt hostility towards a parent, and violent efforts to destroy him, may be the result of feeling that the parent has not accepted one, the other side of the face of love. Ambivalence, however, *as a concept*, has meaning only in terms of its opposite—the representation of ambivalence, as an inherent quality of man, or as a special attribute of a single character, depends upon the implication of its plausible alternative, so that any action of ambivalence can be seen as one of at least two possibilities. So long as the possibility of acting certainly lurks behind the actuality of acting ambivalently, the failure to have acted certainly is open to a number of explanations: weakness, in any one of its manifold forms; failure to understand the reciprocal nature of the relationship between love and hate; dominion of the superego and the death of the ego; too adhesive a cluster of Oedipal feelings; faulty reasoning; faulty assessment of reality; or the human incapacity to transcend the human condition. The ambivalence of Joseph K., however, is none of these. He *is* in a position of ambivalence because of where he finds himself with respect to where he wishes to go. Being shut out, rather than shut in, he must go *back* if he is to move at all; he will achieve "freedom" in its negative form, that of returning to his former place of confinement; it is no longer "good" to be cast out and to be freed from fetters, it is bad, and as traumatic as the casting out from the womb at birth is traumatic. It is a form of freedom which Marjorie Grene, in a completely different context, calls "dreadful,"[16] and which the Angel of Jehovah, coming upon Hagar in the course of her first flight from Sarai, advises her to eschew. It is significant in this connection that after Hagar returns and accepts her condition (successfully completing the voyage *back*) she is cast out again, this time with the advice and consent of God—she enters into involuntary rather than voluntary exile. It may be presumed that God has His reasons, and that these reasons are didactic. In the course of her wanderings as a "free" woman, Hagar almost reaches the ultimate point of failure, symbolized in the story by the exhaustion of the contents of her water skin. In short, as God may have wished to demonstrate, her efforts to survive on her own are hopeless, and her "freedom" is a mirage. Perhaps because He realizes that, having made the mistake of thinking that she could "free" herself by her own actions, Hagar is incapable of understanding, God chooses to talk at this critical juncture in Hagar's affairs not to Hagar but to Ishmael, through whom He reveals the proximity of a suitable water supply. The difference between the two flights would seem to indicate a dimension of futility which underlies the ambivalence of the actions of Joseph K., the futility of human endeavors to compass by human means that which can only be accomplished in accordance with Divine purpose. Thus there is revolt and acceptance, love and hate, which subsist side by side, and which produce ineffectiveness because in a sense they cancel each other out, as Hagar's inability to flee or to return renders her incapable of achieving her freedom. But Joseph K., we have said, is not a revolutionary precisely because of the ambiguity of the revolu-

[16] In the original title of her book: *Dreadful Freedom; A Critique of Existentialism*, Chicago: University of Chicago Press, 1948. The author apparently subsequently lost some of her initial apprehensiveness, for the book was republished in 1959, by the same press, with a new title: *Introduction to Existentialism.*

tionary attitude seen in this fabric of reciprocal and polar tension. To be a revolutionary he must *become* a revolutionary in the same way that he has already *become* ambivalence itself; he must not try to return anywhere but must, by casting aside the notion of return, reposition the present into the present, rather than the implied future. Of course "Joseph K." cannot be expected to do this, since the inability to do this is coeval with that which Joseph K. is. Kafka thus presents us with another inversion, this time of the nature of the revolutionary act, or the act by which freedom can be gained.

Normally, there is implied in the act of revolution the act of turning against and hence of "turning around." But that which is turned around is still the same thing, only this time seen in a different dimension: the revolutionary confirms the condition against which he revolts by pitting himself against it; he offers another version of society, or another distribution of its component parts, or he exchanges rôles with those who have hitherto had a monopoly of them.[17] There is thus no substantive attack and no increase in the distance between the revolter and the situation against which he revolts; it is only a matter of reorganization of the materials. Revolutionary actions, therefore, imply a position to start with which is *within* the organization. But Joseph K. is *outside;* he has already been rejected. If he confines his activities to regaining his former position, if he insists upon being allowed to re-enter, he cannot be revolutionary at all, for this is a possibility which will be open to him only after he has succeeded in re-entering. The desire to re-enter is in itself a sign of the acceptance of

---

[17] This phenomenon can be seen in the growing bourgeoisification of the communist societies, in which the parts formerly played by the entrenched bourgeoisie are now being played, happily, by the children of those who overthrew them. In fact, what used to be bourgeois taste has remained as the taste of the proletariat, *vide* the Victorian character of Soviet architecture and the style of the 1939 Buick as the vehicular beauty most devoutly to be wished.

that which it is desired to re-enter. If it were not so, the desire to re-enter would disappear. It is thus impossible for Joseph K., *in view of where he is*, to revolt, and hence to act certainly, with a clear and purposive objective. The only way in which this could be accomplished would be to recognize that (a) he is outside, and (b) to disaffirm the existence of any other "inside"; in short, to accept the responsibility of full freedom. There would have to be, in the world which K. inhabits, a qualitative change of condition. To ask a condition, however, to be another condition, is absurd; it is equally absurd to expect Joseph K. to undergo this change.[18] Now if true revolutionary action involves such a qualitative change, and such a change is in the nature of the structure of *The Trial* out of the question for Joseph K., his failure to take such action contains its own immanent ambivalence. The only way to get out of a condition of ambivalence is to move into a condition of non-ambivalence, which presupposes the recognition of the unique nature of freedom, and of its responsibility. Thus, as what he is, Joseph K. vacillates between not only the polar pulls of acceptance and rejection, but between their rhetorical expressions. Every proposition stated by him is followed by, in effect, "on the other hand," or by some qualification. The state of being shut out contains its own ambivalence, so that nothing anybody does who is shut out can be other than ambivalent—for the state of being shut out is such a state only so long as one wishes to be let back in, or to be admitted. This is one of the major figures of *The Trial*, and the "Parable of the Law" contains it in special, but not qualitatively different form.

[18] The failure to understand this may be the cause of the impatience of the "YMCA" school of critics, who are constantly annoyed at Kafka for not, in effect, pulling up his socks and getting on with it. Edmund Wilson, often so brilliant, falls into this attitude in his essay "A Dissenting Opinion on Kafka," *New Yorker*, July 26, 1947.

16.

The Priest's Tale

It is not necessary to consider the particular significance of the Law, if indeed it has any, to note that at the beginning of the priest's tale the man is in the position of seeking admission to it, and is thus, by a completely voluntary decision quite free from even implied coercion, outside a condition into which for his own reasons he wishes to be allowed. There is thus no inherent reason why, with respect to the Law, the man should be outside rather than within; he is outside because he wants to go in, because that which is beyond the door has an attraction for him of such an order that he will feel excluded from it until he can cross the threshold. His outsideness, then, derives from the way in which he constitutes himself, and is hence incapable of being disjoined from the man himself, or from any of the actions which he may take. He is the condition, or the state, of outsideness, of exclusion, and it is thus impossible that he should ever be anything else or be able to do anything which will make him "insideness," or, within the framework of the tale, admit him. It is thus clear that when the door-keeper tells him that he may not be admitted at once, he has in effect no alternative but that of waiting, at least so long as he persists in conceiving his position as that of exclusion, for if one waits, one might as well sit down on a stool, which the man does. Among other things, this is on the one hand not a sign that the man is obdurate, patient or even resigned; on the other hand it is not a sign that the man is imbued with a particularly strong desire to be admitted to the Law, that he is, in a manner of speaking, a fanatic. Within the limits of what he is, the man can act only as he does, and his actions, however they may be regarded by the priest or by the commentators to whom the priest refers, have no meaning apart from themselves. Like Joseph K. himself, the man at the door is the essence, and the face, of ambivalence, and it is the nature of ambivalence to paralyze action and to bring about a suspension of movement. It is interesting that the man should come from the country; it may be that "country" signifies to Kafka an area to which the most recent developments have not yet been able to penetrate, so that the older values, in fact obsolete, prevail there anachronistically.

The man is, then, before the door voluntarily, and his decision to remain there when he is informed that he may not be immediately admitted is not a casual one, nor one taken because he sees no other alternative. He obviously understands that it is open to him to return home (to disaffirm the Law), but he rejects this choice in favor of his decision to remain, a decision which he takes "on reflection." Convinced that the Law should be accessible at all times, what disturbs the man most at this point is to find that it is not. The Law, since the man is "going to" it, is conceived by him in terms of its futurity, which he has no reason to doubt; the man is, to his own way of thinking, in the process of arrival, and we have discussed the implications of arrival with respect to the nature and the position of the goal. But the sequence of time is inverted, as are so many of the other sequences in *The Trial*. If the Law represents the actual world, the man, (as K.), is removed from it by an exclusion which places him anterior to the present, so that the present plays the rôle that the future ordinarily plays in, among other areas, traditional religion. When the man expresses surprise and regret that the Law should not be permanently and invariably accessible, he is expressing the confusion which results from learning that the "future" does not lie ahead and that, in consequence, the act of moving "towards" it will not bring it closer, but, indeed, will have the effect of pushing it farther away. This confusion is never resolved by the man; unable to change his interpretation of the position which he occupies, he is unable to do more than engage upon a series of repetitive efforts to achieve his goal, and these efforts vary only in terms of his growing fatigue. They are all ineffective in any case, but they become feebler as time wears on and the man grows older. In much the same way, and for the same reasons, Joseph K. engages in a series of repetitive actions which become harder to accomplish as fatigue sets in, the fatigue not only of growing age, but the fatigue which repetitiveness itself produces. Now during his long wait on the stool the door-keeper does not entirely ignore the man; he converses with him, but on an "impersonal" level. This is another example of the inversion of experience which characterizes the novel, if we consider the circumstance that the subjects which the door-keeper discusses with the man are ordinarily extremely personal in their nature, and if we understand by "personal" their concern with the individual, rather than the general. He enquires about the man's home and other matters concerning his former life, but the impersonality stems from the irrelevancy of these questions, not from their subject matter. For background, social, economic, religious, is customarily conceived as having so intimate a relationship with what a man does that it is assumed that an understanding and an explanation of a man may well emerge from a full dossier on all that he has done and all the relationships that he has had,[19] which implies the causal nature of background which interestingly enough Walt Whitman rejected when, in the course of soliciting an identification with himself as man, he wrote:

[19] It is instructive to note that government agencies, when they wish to satisfy themselves completely about the character of a potential employee, invariably demand a list of the places where he has lived since birth, a complete record of the activities he has engaged in, and other data which are unrelated to his quality as a man.

The Priest's Tale

Trippers and askers surround me,
People I meet, the effect upon me of my early life
or the ward and city I live in, or the nation . . .[20]

Whitman knows that ". . . they are not the Me myself," and so
in effect does the door-keeper. Since they are not, his questions
are asked "impersonally." Kafka explains that the questions
are put impersonally "as great men put questions"; greatness
may be a quality of knowing the true significance of what one
says, and if no question of this sort can be relevant in the
nature of things, knowledge of this irrelevancy would make
it impossible for a great man to put one in any other way.
The delusion that such questions have point may well be one
of the signs of being excluded from the world; a figure, in
other ways, of the state of incomprehension. Such questions
would of course be relevant if the Law were, as the man thinks
it is, a culmination, if it represented "paradise," admission to
which is gained by works—in short, if the Law were a statement of process and pattern. But when there is no culminative
element, the questions become the form of questions, emptied
of their relevance and, like the universe which it may be
presumed that they reflect, impersonal.

During the course of his years of waiting, the man attempts
various ways of gaining admittance, including the offer of
bribes to the door-keeper. This offer of bribes, of which an
early example in *The Trial* is K.'s attempt to buy off the
whipper, is characteristic of the efforts made by K., in fact
and by implication, to secure his freedom from the operations
of the law. It is, of course, an assumption of corruption, and
it is based upon the conviction that what has happened is
merely a fateful and unhappy accident, having no larger
meaning, the effects of which can be modified by bribing a
deflection. In a sense bribery is the only means open to those
who, finding themselves enmeshed in the toils of a system which
is so remote from them that they are unable to comprehend

[20] Stanza 4 of *Song of Myself*.

it, can react only to its external and immediate manifestation, which they take, in the absence of additional knowledge of understanding, to be the system itself. For this reason the officer of the law is seen as the law itself, and Joseph K., after he is first arrested, finds it difficult to comprehend what the warders are trying to tell him, that they are only minor officials who are carrying out a task, and not the system itself, so that it is useless to attempt to dissuade them from the completion of their duties. The crime, in this context, becomes that of having been unfortunate enough to have been arrested, not the act itself. The punishment which may follow is thus punishment for having been arrested, and this, as we have seen, is one of the inversions which inform the novel. But when punishment is only punishment for having been arrested, the source of it would appear to be the arresting official who, since it is thought that he made the arrest only because he happened to come along at that time, may presumably be diverted elsewhere by the introduction of a suitable inducement. Bribery is a function of the distance which exists between the operative elements of a system and the system itself, a distance which in turn is a function of the degree to which the people within the system understand it; at the lower levels of understanding, and hence at the lower levels of the officialdom, bribery alone is effective, and even then, only partially so. The difficulty which ensues is that when bribery fails, because, for example, the bribe is refused, it is natural to conclude that it failed because the inducement was inadequate, or because it was offered to the wrong person, or offered improperly (it will be recalled that K., when he thinks of bribing the whipper, consults his wallet furtively). The fact that it cannot work at all is of course not understood; as a result, repeated efforts are made, differing only in inconsequential detail. Bribery implies not only ignorance of the system, and the confusion of its parts with the whole, but constitutes a statement that there

is no purpose, only chance, so that concentration is upon
means and means alone, upon process as process rather than
upon process as related to principle. This is perhaps why in
daily morality bribery is thought of as being an unprincipled
activity. It may, however, be the only effective activity in a
world in which there is no principle. Certainly even the officials
of the Court recognize this; in the achievement of ostensible
acquittal, for example, it is always understood that influence
is important. Punishment is thus seen, when bribery fails, as
evidence of a failure to have found the proper means, or to
have used them properly; it is hence deserved for one thing,
for another it is never justified. There thus develops a fundamental ambiguity of acceptance and rejection, seen best in an
earlier context in Oedipus, who never really fully accepts the
justice of his blindness and exile and remains crustily of two
minds about them all the way to Colonnus. The efforts of
the man to bribe the door-keeper thus embody one aspect
of the efforts of Joseph K. to bribe the universe, and stem
from the same set of misdirected assumptions. But the door-
keeper does not refuse the bribes; on the contrary he accepts
them "to keep you," as he puts it to the man, "from feeling
you have left something undone." In this attitude the door-
keeper may have put his finger on the heart of the problem for
Joseph K., who until the knife ends his life, never ceases to
worry lest there be something that he failed to do, lest even the
repetitive actions and their repeated innocuity, if only continued another round or two, should not somehow end in a
victory. The trouble is, of course, that the man sees only the
need for another bribe, not the futility of bribes.

It occurs to the man, but apparently only after an interminable period of time, that he has not in all those endless
years seen another person coming to the door to ask to be
admitted, and with his failing breath he puts this single and
climactic insight into a question to the door-keeper, whose

113

response is that the door was intended only for him. The door is a door to the extent that the man postulates it as a door, that is, as an entrance to, and a threshold of, another world which lies beyond. So long as the door is there, and so long as it is a door under these conditions, it cannot be the door of anybody else, that is, it has no intrinsic "doorness" apart from its denomination as a door by the man. Doors of this order are unique; they cannot be shared, and they keep the man "out" because he affirms his "outness" by affirming the desirability of going "in." The barrier that constitutes the symbol of his "outness" is self-conceived, and entirely self-conceived, and cannot therefore have ever been "intended" for anybody else, so that the door-keeper, who has had the reciprocal function, and no other, of keeping the door, must always have been designated to keep the door for this one man. He is not a door-keeper in general, a sharer of professional qualifications with other door-keepers, but a keeper of a single door, a single function which is inseparable both from the door he keeps and from the man who makes it possible for him to keep it by investing it with its door-like qualities. It follows therefore that with the death of the man there must be a corresponding death of the door-keeper, who is now left without function and hence without identity. For this reason he shuts the door, or rather, he banishes it by removing from it its capacity to serve as entrance. It becomes one with a continuous barrier at a point where there may be no further "beyond," because the affirmative power which created this "beyond" has died coevally with the man.

It is this story for which the priest offers a gloss to K. The act of offering a gloss at all implies that the story has layers of meaning; indeed, the priest refers to "commentators" who have based their own careful work of interpretation upon the assumption that the text contains meaning. It would thus appear at first to be a question of what the meaning is, and K., understanding this aspect of the telling of the tale, responds appropriately by suggesting a tentative one, that the door-keeper apparently deluded the man. But the rhetorical structure of the priest's reply deserves attention because it is the same as the rhetorical structure of earlier examples in the novel of the ineffective sputtering out which follows careful analysis. It is once again cast in the form and texture of the fizzle, similar to that which ensues from the conversation with Fräulein Montag or from the careful consideration of the proposition that the whole affair of the initial arrest is some sort of rather monstrous joke. As can be said of K.'s first appearance before the Examining Magistrate, that he tells the Magistrate absolutely everything he knows about his case and thus tells him nothing, the priest tells K. absolutely everything he knows about the meaning of the story and ends by telling him nothing. For K. offers the conclusion that the story indicates that the door-keeper deluded the man because he gave him the message of salvation (that the door was never intended for anybody except him) too late, that is, too late to be helpful to the man, who is too close to the end of his life for it to matter any more. The priest responds to this conclusion of K.'s by offering two explanations of the door-keeper's conduct, one substantive, the other not. The reply is in two parts. *First* the priest says "He was not asked the question any earlier," to which he appends a further answer, that the door-keeper "fulfilled his duty." Now the first answer is substantive because it can lead to a fruitful discussion of the moral question involved as to whether or not there was any obligation on the part of the door-keeper to give the message before being asked, which implies that (a) there are such things as moral obligations; (b) that the door-keeper's conduct may be judged in accordance with these standards; (c) that if it is determined that he should have given the message before being asked, he is therefore a "bad" door-keeper and K. is right in thinking that the essence of the story lies in the fact that the man was deluded; and (d) that if indeed no moral obligation weighed upon the door-keeper to give the message of salvation in advance of the question, he is not therefore a "bad" door-keeper, and the man cannot be his victim, so that K.'s conclusion is erroneous. All of this further implies that there are statements which may be applied to door-keepers in general, applicable to the particular door-keeper to the extent that he is a member of the class "door-keepers" and shares a certain number of their characteristics, so that he is presumed to have a function of keeping doors in general and to have in consequence that disjunction between man and function which makes it possible to assign "him" elsewhere within the general limitations of his profession, or to ascribe to him a weakness in the performance of his duties which must be his own weakness,[21] not that of the duties themselves. But the door-keeper kept only the one door and kept it for the particular man; he is not discrete from his function any more than the man is from his. K. is thus blocked in the first place from considering the significance of the door-keeper's act because the act and the door-keeper are indivisible. He is blocked further, however, by his own structural ambivalence: he chooses to respond, not to the substantive answer which the priest offers, but to the irrelevant answer, that the door-keeper "fulfilled his duty." He thus begins by placing himself at an additional remove from the basic issue, and confronts, with the analytical apparatus of his logical mind, an irrelevancy which cannot be clarified because it is an irrelevancy. The priest seizes upon this and suggests a further qualification in answer to K.'s clearly implied doubt that the door-keeper was fulfilling his duty. He states that as a matter of fact it is more accurate to say that he was not fulfilling his duty, but exceeding it, although not exceeding it very much.

[21] In fact, the priest later advances the suggestion that the door-keeper is "a little simple-minded and consequently a little conceited."

This is parallel to the nature of the discussion between K. and the Inspector on the question of whether or not K. was surprised or very surprised, and proceeds in the same manner. The priest offers a most comprehensive and logical series of deductions from the scripture itself to justify his conclusion that the door-keeper was exceeding his duty rather than fulfilling it. Among the reasons he gives are the fact that the door-keeper leaves the possibility of later admission open when he first meets the man, that he keeps the door without relaxation and shuts it only when he must, that he is incorruptible, and that his appearance hints at a "pedantic" character. This has much the aspect of Fräulein Montag's report of Fräulein Bürstner's presumed views of the nature of interviews, and is equally doomed to be sterile of effective or productive results. If by "analysis" we mean not only the method but its relevancy to that which is being analyzed, it can be seen that the reasoning of the priest in this instance is only the form of analysis, not analysis itself, for the matter of concern is already at several removes and is untouched.

The inherent inapplicability of the rhetorical structure is disclosed in still another aspect of the priest's argumentation, in that section where he appears to be dealing with the question of whether the man is more free than the door-keeper or less so. For this argument depends upon the deliberate severance, by the priest, of two interwoven elements: the freedom of the door-keeper and the freedom of the man, with the implication that while it is possible to argue that one is freer than the other, there is no reason to assume that the greater freedom of the one can have been achieved without the corresponding lessening of the freedom of the other. That there is such a condition as that of freedom goes without saying in the implication of the argument; further, it goes without saying that no freedom is absolute, but is limited to a greater or lesser extent. Two individuals conceived, as are the man and the

door-keeper within the tale, as occupying reciprocal positions
with respect to each other which are distinguished by the
extent of these limitations upon absolute freedom, are in
consequence capable of serving as symbols of their relative
freedom—one is less free because he has more limitations, or
more free because he has fewer. Within these assumptions,
the kind of evidence which the priest brings to bear upon the
argument is relevant and may in fact even be useful. The conclusion he comes to, however, is not functionally important;
he can conclude that one is freer than the other, or the other
freer than the one, without affecting the process of the evaluation. It is thus an error to feel melancholy, as does K.,
because the final conclusion of the priest is other than that
which K. would apparently wish to have demonstrated, which
presupposes that K. would not have felt melancholy if the
priest had allowed his arguments to lead to the opposite
conclusion. In fact, if K. is to feel melancholy "realistically,"
or "justifiably," he should feel melancholy in the face of either
conclusion, because of the failure of the method itself. But the
entire process of the priest's argumentation is doomed to failure
if only because, in using the two men as symbols of their relative freedom, he is forced inevitably to argue the subject of
relative freedom, a subject which is in itself irrelevant, and
indeed absurd, in a universe where freedom is absolute. The
disjunction of the two men which underlies the argument of
the priest falsifies their permanent and inextricable fusion. For
the man is free to go, to return if he wishes to his home, to
wander about as he chooses; there is only one place that is
barred to him, the territory beyond the door. The door-keeper
is not free to leave his post and in that sense is less free than
the man. But the man persists in remaining camped before the
door and in giving the door-keeper something to do as well
as a door to keep, and to that extent he is not free to go, or
rather the fact that he is free to go is purely theoretical, an

alternative which has no validity so long as it is not taken. As a result, at any given time in the long years, the man is as much bound to his post as the door-keeper is to his. The man is at his post because he is the condition of petition, the door-keeper is at his because he is the condition of keeping the door; so long as the man wishes to enter, the door-keeper will keep him out, and so long as he is kept out, the door-keeper will have a greater freedom than the man insofar as he is in and the man is out. The man can be free only if he *accepts* his freedom: his bondage is a function of his unwillingness or his incapacity to do so. He confers the greater freedom upon the door-keeper by investing the territory beyond the door with the characteristic of being desirable to enter, and in doing so, lessens his own. The door-keeper's service was, as the priest remarks, an "empty formality" until the man arrived to seek admittance. It would continue to be an empty formality if the man never came, or having come, turned away and accepted his freedom. Thus there can be no severance of the freedom of the two men: it is indivisible. Each is absolutely free; neither can accept his absolute freedom; each places himself in a relative position with respect to the other, and the freedom is seen as relative. But it is not, and the argument is inherently fated to end in no substantive understanding of the nature of the experience.

The exegeses of the priest must fail to arrive at a meaning in a situation which contains none, and which imposes upon him the use of exegetical tools which relate to another universe of discourse. K. is sensitive to this, and mourns what he takes to be the impossibility of arriving at ultimate truth. The priest, however, makes a suggestion which K. is no more able to follow at this late point in his life than he was at the beginning of the novel, that "it is not necessary to accept everything as true, one must only accept it as necessary." This is a plea, in a way, by the priest for acting "as if" there were universal truths, for doing away with the necessity which plagues K. of having the further conviction that the truths indeed have some sort of separate and independent existence or universal validity.[22] A convention may in fact be only a convention: it may be argued that it is only when one recognizes that a convention is only a convention that one can follow it, that while the absence of a universality to truth may imply that man has no control over his fate, it also implies that nothing else does. For K. differs in this respect from the others in the novel. He always wants to know more, and like the man before the door, peers and tries to get glimpses when full views are not available. The others do not do this: the door-keeper would not dare to look further than the third keeper, who has an aspect he "cannot bear to look at"; the clients and petitioners who infest the areas of the Court do not even wish to make an attempt to see, much less consult, the "Great Advocates"; in *The Castle* K. is distinguished by his insistence on knowing more about the castle, of which the others remain in voluntary and blessed ignorance. An understanding of the philosophy of "as if" is perhaps the answer to a question which Joseph K. asks himself only fleetingly and almost as if he has of its importance only the merest hint, as evanescent as that hint which he may have had when he told the Examining Magistrate that the trial was only a trial if he recognized it as such. He wonders, as he first sees the priest in the cathedral, whether the priest might not indicate to him the way, "not towards some influential manipulation of the case, but towards a circumvention of it, a getting rid of it altogether, a mode of living completely outside the jurisdiction of the Court." The Court might well lose jurisdiction if it is itself only the abstraction of the postulation, not of any particular truth, but of universal truth in general; it

---

[22] It is curious that Eliseo Vivas should have concluded that the priest was trying to convey to K. the message that he should have "genuine contrition." *Vide* his "Kafka's Distorted Mask," *Kenyon Review*, X, Winter (1948).

would certainly cease to be a world to be sought or to be entered, and it could no longer retain the power of granting petitions. Such a conclusion might indeed be, as K. says it is when he responds to the priest, "melancholy"; but it may also be the one conclusion which has within it the possibility of affording to K. the change of venue without which he must die. But K. cannot do this; he cannot perceive in the answer of the priest even a connection to that answer which at the beginning he hoped, however feebly, to elicit. Instead, he finds the priest's conclusion "melancholy" for a reason which confirms him in his inability to find an answer, that it "turns lying into a universal principle."

A lie, however, is only an untruth, and lying only the telling of falsehoods. The pejorative attributes which lying has, in K.'s response and in the normative moral world, stem from the postulation of truth in the first place, and from, in the second, a conviction that, truth being conceived as coeval with rightness, lying is wrong. Joseph K. has not surrendered his conviction that there is a truth, he has not achieved an ability to face up to the possibility that chaos is the only order, and hence he can see in what the priest says only the conclusion, "melancholy" of course, that he is being asked to consider a world which is wrong. But in a world in which all meaning is subjective and indivisible from the actions in which it occurs, lying is indeed a universal principle, for it is the only way to tell the truth.

Thus the problems of exclusion which are the basis for the story of the priest's tale represent a major configuration of the entire novel, and the restatement of the condition of ambivalence. But the priest's tale functions in this connection in a structural way; it is offered as, and appears to be, a parable. As a matter of fact it is often referred to in critical essays as the "Parable of the Law," and critics (like the priest) treat is as such, open to interpretation, commentary, conclusion, argumentation and logical analysis. To Martin Buber, for example, it is the "Parable of the man who squanders his life before a certain open gateway which leads to the world of meaning."[23] The man, Buber notices, is not in a condition to know that the door is open to him. Buber, of course, knows this very well, and would presumably not have "squandered" his own life. He goes on to assure us that the parable is not Pauline, but that "its elaborations are. [It is] concerned with the judgment under which the soul stands and under which it places itself willingly." Nor does Clemens Heselhaus, in his "Kafkas Erzahlformen," doubt that he is dealing with parable. In fact, he assigns it the essential rôle in the novel.[24] K.'s error quite possibly lies in seeing the story of the priest as a parable; certainly his ultimate discomfort is due to the fact that he thinks it fails to clarify as much as a parable should, and the discomfort of many critics derives from what must surely be the obscurity of the parable, if parable it be. It is, however, the essence of the quality of parables that they should "relate" to something outside of themselves; they are fictive representations of relationships, truths, and patterns which have their own external, and hence "true" existence. Parables are in this sense reflective and symbolic of discourses of experience, much like the language itself in which they are conveyed, and they consequently, in their own nature, suggest order and depend upon order. This is no less true, obviously, when the order is remote or obscure; remoteness and obscurity only goad the commentator to further frenzied attacks on the bast fibres which conceal the nut. But in a world of no order and of no universal, *a priori* truths, there can in effect be no parables. Such "parables" as exist are no longer parables at all, but their *form*. Once again we are confronted in *The Trial* with the desuetude of form deprived of content; the implica-

[23] *Two Types of Faith*, trans. Norman P. Goldhawk. London: Routledge and Kegan Paul, Ltd., 1957, p. 165.

[24] *Deutsche Vierteljahresschrift für Litteraturwissenschaft Geistesgeschichte*, XXVI:3, Tübingen, 1952.

tion that the content has disappeared; the further implication therefore that the form relates only to the past; the further implication that since it does, an attempt to use it or to give it flesh can only be a backward movement which itself has the form of forward progress; and the particular nature and face of the essential futility which must result. The "parable" of the Law functions only as the paradigm of parable, not as parable itself, and this paradigm is a complete paradigm, in microcosm, of the paradigm which *The Trial* is as novel.

I 7.

Energy and Action "as If"

"To ask questions," K. thinks as he reviews his dissatisfaction with the services of the advocate Huld, "was surely the main thing," and to K. it never fails to be the main thing. Unlike the other people connected with the Court, K. has a compulsive need to know more. He insists upon further explanations and further answers, and demands, in addition, that these answers should be clear and unambiguous. While he "knows" that he is not guilty, he must have a clearcut statement of his innocence. The "ostensible" acquittal of which the painter speaks, or the indefinite postponement, are more repugnant to K. than what he would take to be an unjustified conviction. K. is, as we have noted before, distinguished in this wise from those with whom he suddenly finds himself, a distinction which may be the nature, or an aspect of the nature, of his alienation and, if alienation is a form of guilt, of his guilt. To use the lesson of Hamlet in another context, K. wants either to be or not to be; for him, that is the question. His overwhelming desire to be leads him to enquire endlessly about the nature of the world in which alone this being can occur. The question, however, of "to be or not to be" implies that each is the alternative, and the sole alternative, of the other. But we have suggested already that in fact Joseph K. may be considered to be suspended in a limbo between being and not being. He has certainly ceased to be in the sense that he "was" prior to his arrest; he has not as yet succeeded in being in the sense of acceptance into the world from which he has been expelled. The very form, therefore, of the question, with its two mutually exclusive categories, falsifies the position and gives to the ultimate resolution of the question a permanent futility. What Joseph K. does not take into consideration is that instead of two positions with respect to man's relationship to existence, there may be four, on the order described by Unamuno:

Hay, en efecto, cuatro posiciones, que son dos positivas: a) querer ser; b) querer no ser; y dos negativas: c) no querer ser; d) no querer no ser.[25]

[25] Miguel de Unamuno y Jugo, *Tres Novelas Ejemplares y un Prólogo*, Madrid: Espasa-Calpe, S.A. (Colleción Contemporánea) n.d., p. 16.

As a matter of fact, there may be six. Oliver Wendell Holmes, (*op. cit.*, p. 53) outlines them as follows with respect to a conversation between John and Thomas:

Three Johns.
1. The real John; known only to his Maker.
2. John's ideal John; never the real one, and often very unlike him.
3. Thomas's ideal John; never the real John, nor John's John, but often very unlike either.

Three Thomases.
1. The real Thomas.
2. Thomas's ideal Thomas.
3. John's ideal Thomas.

Holmes continues: "It follows, that, until a man can be found who knows himself as his Maker knows him, or who sees himself as others see him, there must be at least six persons engaged in every dialogue between two."

Energy and Action "as If"

The traditional "hero" insists upon the set of positive positions, to wish to be or to wish not to be. Indeed he must, if he is to function as "hero" within the traditional framework of the literary process. Unamuno discusses this problem in these terms:

Como se puede: creer que hay Dios, creer que no hay Dios, no creer que hay Dios y no creer que no hay Dios. Y ni creer que no hay Dios es lo mismo que no creer que hay Dios, ni querer no ser es no querer ser. De uno que no quiere ser difícilmente se saca una criatura poética, de novela; pero de uno que quiere no ser, sí. Y el que quiere no ser, no es . . . un suicida.[26]

It is the common people who are content with the negative ones, not to want to be and not to want not to be; as a matter of fact it is this which often distinguishes the common from the uncommon. The "negative" attitudes are negative only in a discourse where there are external, stable values. In an existential universe, far from being negative, they are positive, and they characterize the attitudes of all the persons in the area of the Court with the exception of K. They represent a form of acceptance which does not imply, as K. evidently thinks, and as many readers assume, an aspect of resignation which makes all action useless. Not to want to be and not to want not to be rather imply that "being" is not a primary goal as such, but only a necessary one, and that this understood, it is not unimportant to attempt to affect the particular nature of existence as best one can, to work, in other words, within the system without feeling the obligation of postulating either that the system is "right" or that it relates to a universal truth. Life may well be contingent, but if it is it may be wiser not to look too far for its ultimate meanings. As Malherbe wrote:

[26] *Op. cit.*, pp. 16–17.

Non qu'il ne me soit grief que la terre possède
    Ce qui me fut si cher;
Mais en un accident qui n'a point de remède,
    Il n'en faut point chercher.

And the members of the world of the Court may understand
this, and realize the necessity which Malherbe offers, in the
last stanza, as the only source of solace:

De murmurer contre elle et perdre patience
    Il est mal à propos;
Vouloir ce que Dieu veut est la seule science
    Qui nous met en repos.[27]

Malherbe wrote "met" and not "mette" in the last line, for he
knows this beyond doubt. It is thus "scientific" to ask questions, possibly stupid not to, but the questions must be of a
different kind from those which K. wishes that the advocate
would continue to ask—they must be aimed at finding out not
what the Court "means," but how the Court operates, in order
to be able to work effectively within the context. Dr. Huld
makes a great point of how important it is that the accused,
who is usually distracted, should have the assistance of somebody who knows what to do. He refers to the information
which he is often able to glean from unexpected visits to his
office by Court officials, and says that the chief value of the
defense lies in the personal connections the advocate may have
with the Court. He goes on to say that the first plea, although
it is difficult to draw it up when the charge itself is unknown,
none the less has a great bearing upon the progress of the
case, and that in one way or another the proceedings may be
influenced, "imperceptibly at first, perhaps, but more and
more strongly" as the case goes on. In short there are, in Dr.
Huld's view, steps which may be taken. Indeed, it would be
folly not to take these steps, since they are, to begin with, the

[27] From *Consolation à Monsieur Du Périer, Gentilhomme d'Aix en
Provence, sur la mort de sa fille.*

only steps which are capable of having a possible result, and while it is true that they may have none, it is also true that unless they should be taken, no possibility remains of achieving any effect at all. Dr. Huld understands that in the higher reaches of the Court it may turn out that everything he has done will prove to have been futile: officials who in a private chat have indicated a view favorable to the defense "might well go straight to their offices and issue a statement in the directly contrary sense." But he concludes in effect that it is important to act *as if* what one was doing were relevant. Such actions must, in the words of the priest, be understood as being necessary rather than true. The difference between many of the accused and those who tried to help them, and certainly the difference which marks Joseph K., is that they have a "passion for suggesting reforms which often wasted time and energy which could have been better employed in other directions." There is no point either in trying to alter details or in being concerned with the universality of the meaning of the Court. Huld sums it up by telling K. that "the only sensible thing was to adapt oneself to conditions." It is not a question of not wanting to be or not wanting not to be, but of arranging the particular conditions of this limbo in the most advantageous possible way. In a sense, of course, Huld's conclusion suggests resignation, but it is a resignation to the necessary limits of existence and does not imply an actual passivity. In fact, the realization on the part of the inhabitants of the world of the Court of the impossibility, and the undesirability, of probing for further knowledge and absolute meaning, is precisely what gives them, in contradistinction to K., a great deal of energy. None of the people with whom K. comes into contact shares the fatigue with which his insistence upon absolutes is bound to afflict him. He might do well to heed Malherbe's words to Alcandre, and find his cure, from "pensées lassées" at least,

Que n'êtes-vous lassées,
Mes tristes pensées,
De troubler ma raison,
Et faire avecque blâme
Rebeller mon âme
Contre ma guérison?[28]

in the recognition that his "justes requêtes" will obtain no answer, perhaps because they are not really just at all. While the world of the Court may appear to go nowhere and to engage in repetitively useless activity, its population is busy, energetic and constantly working to accomplish something within the realm of the necessary. Huld pursues his clients' interests with assiduity, and takes advantage of every opportunity, however slight, which comes his way to modify the course of events. He will apply his intelligence to the drawing of a plea or make use of his personal contacts to see to it that the plea is favorably received. His fellow advocates, thrown down the stairs by an irate official who is tired of having his consideration of a case interrupted by a series of petitions, do not passively accept this ignominious defeat; on the contrary, they consider the nature of the problem and determine to do something about it in their self-interest. They recognize, however, the essential nature of their problem, that they have no *right* to enter the official's office. They are not outraged, while K., deluded that he has rights, expresses his outrage at their having been trampled and finds that his indignation, however beautifully expressed, is ineffective. It is precisely this failure to understand that he has no rights that leads him to that fatigue which is the product of Sisyphus-like labors. The advocates, however, recognizing that they have no right to enter the office, do not conclude that for that reason they have no right to want to. As a matter of fact, their expulsion from the office is a serious matter to them, since "every day they spent

---

[28] From the fourth *Stances pour Alcandre*.

away from the Court was a day lost to them." The acceptance
of their position does not carry with it the additional obligation
of being pleased with it, nor does it imply that because they
have no rights they should not act as if they did, in order to
better their immediate lot if it is possible to do so. So they take
counsel with each other and decide upon a course of action,
to tire out the official by sending up one advocate after another
for him to throw down. In the course of time the old official in
fact becomes weary and the advocates, somewhat to their own
surprise, find that they may enter the office freely. It is thus
not fair to assume that the advocates do nothing, nor even that
they do nothing substantive; this latter conclusion is the
product of the hypothesis that there is a transcendental truth
and that a relationship to it is the only measure of the sub-
stantiveness of an action.

Nor is Leni incapable of action. K. himself notices that she
has a good knowledge about the Court and its intrigues, she
obviously knows her way around, and although she occupies a
low position in her social hierarchy, she has a sufficient understanding of procedure not only to acquit herself usefully in
her own place, but to offer some help to K. She can advise him,
for example, that it would be well to make an early confession,
and can identify the source of his ineffectiveness in his being
too unyielding. "But must you eternally be brooding over
your case?" she asks K., and then counsels him: "take my
warning to heart instead, and don't be so unyielding in future,
you can't put up a resistance against this Court, you must
admit your fault. Make your confession at the first chance
you get." Her words are misunderstood by K., who is unwilling
to confess as a matter of procedure, only as a matter of justice,
and who cannot do so unless he thinks that he has something to
confess, as a crime of which he is guilty. Leni does not imply,
nor is there evidence that she presupposes, that there must be
any ultimate justification for confession. Confession is a useful

act in circumstances where without it no further progress can be made; it may in fact yield no results, but it may also lead, if not to a permanent relief, to a certain amelioration. It is at any rate an open path, failure to take which will inevitably be disastrous. K., unwilling though he is to conceive of confession as a purely useful act, is none the less able to perceive that confession may be a price which Leni, for reasons which are not clear to him, wishes to exact in exchange for her help. Her help is thus seen by K. as disjunctive from her advice when in reality it is not, and when Leni assents to K.'s "experimental" question, "And if I don't make a confession of guilt, then you can't help me?" Leni sees through to the heart of the matter: "But you don't in the least want my help, it doesn't matter to you, you're stiff-necked and never will be convinced."

K. is never free from the suspicion of ulterior motive. For example, he thinks that while the advocate's explanations of what he is doing are all well and good, they may in fact really be designed to conceal the circumstance that he has done nothing or, more importantly, may be designed to lull him into an acceptance of his condition which will make it easier for the Court to spring upon him with a sudden verdict to which, because he has been asleep, he will be able to offer no effective defense. He is unable to accept the face value of things, yet the things with which he comes into contact may have only their face values and be nothing but their face values, without ulterior significance. To conceive of "ulterior" motives is to postulate motives which are not ulterior, which is to say motives which are nothing further than what they appear to be. This is the same order of reaction to the nature of motives as the reaction to the nature of phenomena: in both cases there is presumed to be an ulterior reality of which the appearance may be a falsification. If we consider that in the circumstances there is nothing else that either the advocate or Leni can in fact do, it is futile to weigh their actions against those other actions which it is deemed plausible that they might have done. As we pointed out earlier, the plausible alternative is abolished in a world where actions have no meanings apart from themselves. K., of course, insisting upon the possibility of ulterior motive, moves to the conclusion that in a world of potential scoundrels, corrupt and inefficient mountebanks who hide their selfish concerns behind a mask of hypocritical activity, it is not possible to trust anybody but oneself, the one "person" in whom it is reasonable to have trust. At the conclusion of his lengthy exposure to the advocate's explanations, K. thus decides that it is "absolutely necessary . . . to intervene personally. . . . he must look to himself." This position has a number of difficulties. At the least it denies the nature of the condition of K. by disjoining his self from his awareness of his self and thus, by implication, disjoining the man K. from the function K. To decide that one must "look to oneself" is to assume that it is possible not to look to oneself, which implies that there is either someone else or someplace else available to look to, and that the choice is open. K. thus vacillates between two irrelevant alternatives, whether to trust himself or to trust others, in a context in which the question of trust has no bearing at all, but rather is a question of that kind of inherent responsibility which is the concomitant of the independence which comes through the circumstance of standing alone and without buttress. This decision also implies that there is a self to look to whose nature can be observed disjunctively, and K. proceeds to do just that by summing up the characteristics of that self which "he" now considers to be important to its new job of serving as a prop: he had been successful in working himself up to a good position in the bank, and "if the abilities which had made this possible were to be applied in unravelling his own case, there was no doubt that it would go well." So he has a self not only to look to, but to look to with more than an ordinary hope that it will serve "him" well. It can in any case not be suspected of working for ulterior reasons. To the plea by Leni that it is essential to the progress of his case that he admit his guilt quickly, K. now responds, in effect, by deciding that on the contrary "he should eliminate from his mind the idea of possible guilt." Rejecting the help of Leni, he rejects the help of the advocate and determines not only to represent himself in the ensuing legal actions but to represent himself so forcefully that the Court "would encounter for once an accused man who knew how to stick up for his rights." Unlike the advocates who at least succeeded in entering the office from which they were excluded, K. does not accept the possibility that he has no rights. He now decides on what appears to him to be a forceful defense of his rights, so forceful that it will make the Court sit up and take notice, but incapable of achieving his goal, less capable, in fact, than the simplistic suggestions of the far from intellectual Leni.

On the surface this order of decision seems to be able to infuse K. with a spurt of energy, but this energy quickly becomes fatigue when he realizes all of the difficulties which now confront him, and the enormous task he has set himself in undertaking his own defense. His energy is fleeting because it is false; the energy of Leni and the advocate, on the other hand, continues because it is effective within the limitations of their understanding of necessity. And they are not the only energetic characters. Titorelli is certainly able to paint, and has indeed managed to paint a large number of pictures; there can be no doubt cast upon his ability to function as painter. The fact surprises K. that all of Titorelli's paintings are the same, not merely similar studies, but identical studies, the same "heathscape" on every canvas. Titorelli tells K. that he has painted dozens of them in his time and brings out more examples from under the bed. A painter is somebody who paints as a whipper is somebody who whips, and there is no reason to expect the painter to exercise towards what he paints any more discrimination than the whipper exercises towards the person he whips. In the one case nothing more is required than the function which is achieved through the application of brush to canvas, and the subject, being irrelevant, might just as well be the same (in fact it is probably easier if it is the same, since a certain skill can be developed after much practice); in the other case the function is achieved through the application of whip to body, and the subject of the whipping, being irrelevant, might just as well be the same. In fact, the Whipper continues to whip Franz, in the same sequence, and with the same result, indefinitely. He produces as many identical whipped Franzes as Titorelli produces identical heathscapes, and for the same reason. But neither in the case of the Whipper nor in that of Titorelli is there, as a result, a diminution of energy; on the contrary, the energy is precisely inexhaustible because it is repetitive. But its repetitiveness is not of the same order as the fatiguing repetitiveness which characterizes K., for it does not lead to futility: it cannot, since function and being are identical and fused, with the result that function can only lead to a reaffirmation of being, and thus becomes a life force, or a source of energy. When function and being are discrete, as they appear to be to K., then it becomes the aim of function to achieve being, to bridge a gap which cannot be bridged because it does not exist. In the one case the energy remains, in the other it peters out and is very quickly supplanted by inanition.

Titorelli is not only able to function as a painter, but can sell his paintings with vigor. He can overcome without trouble the weak objections of his customer, K., load his client with goods and thus manage, in a purely economic way, to support himself. His painting is not only function in the abstract, it is function which has the additional quality of enabling him to live from it. He is able to handle the omnipresent girls with aplomb and efficiency. Their presence often irks him, but he finds a way out of his difficulty by expelling them when necessary and trying to keep the door locked when he can. Moreover, since he is painter, he paints despite conditions which would seem to militate against it—the cramped room, the incursions, the lack of space, light or air—not because he overcomes difficulties as such, but because, living/functioning, he paints. His painting, and hence his authority to live, is authorized in certain ways; he is told what to paint, and he cannot, for example, paint the Judge in any other manner than the one which is required, without running the risk of having his passport to life withdrawn. For choice of subject implies, once again, a disjunction between man and function. The artist presumably has an infinite number of choices and he makes one out of all of these. His work can therefore be judged as representing at a minimum not only what he has chosen to paint, but what he has chosen not to paint: the three-dimensional Christ of Renaissance painting certainly constitutes a rejection of the flat Christ of the mediaeval schools. Nor is Titorelli's energy confined to his painting alone. From it he seems to be able to derive additional strength, enough to make it possible for him to have considered the nature of the Court, to communicate his evaluations of it to K., and to make what are to him fruitful recommendations. He does not really defend the Court except against the obvious stupidity of actually questioning it, but it is clear that he, like everybody else, fetches his life and being from it.[29]

The energy which informs the world of the Court is productive not only of activity in general but of sophisticated

[29] Uyttersprot, *op. cit.*, holds that the episode with Titorelli was to be expanded in some further version of the novel. He recognizes that Titorelli, as a clear example of an "initiate," has an especially important function.

understanding of conditions as well. Dr. Huld, for example, is not put off by the pattern of inversion with which he has to deal; on the contrary, he is ready, and able, to put it to its fullest advantage. He has discovered that the advocate requires the client in order to gain some knowledge of the Court, rather than the other way around. As he explains matters to K., the advocate, not normally being allowed to attend the actual proceedings, can learn about them only from a careful questioning of his client immediately after the sessions are over, and can sometimes in consequence hope to piece together something that might be of some use for the defense. The advocate is thus never in a position where he can confront the evidence directly; he must do the best he can to come to correct conclusions on the basis of indirect evidence furnished to him in the form of testimony from the accused, who at least has been at the hearing in person. The extent to which this testimony is helpful in arriving at a useful understanding depends not only upon the acuity of the observation and memory of the accused, but upon the skill with which the advocate elicits it by cross-examination, a skill which varies, obviously, from advocate to advocate. The accuracy of the evidence, and the utility of any plan for the defense which is based upon it, are hence subject to a number of variables over which the advocate has little or no control. None the less, no other course is open to him and he pursues it with as much integrity as he can. Indeed, he would take it unkindly if his activities were to be impeached on this basis alone.[30] Huld under-

[30] When, in November 1966, the photographs and original autopsy reports, made at the time of President Kennedy's assassination, were formally deposited by his family in the national archives, it was reported that the Warren Commission which had investigated the slaying had not ever seen them, but had relied for its opinion about them upon the testimony of the doctors who had made them. It was further stated that the Commission had not thought that it would have had any other opinion if it had in fact seen the original evidence; on the

stands that he has no right to know what transpires at a hearing. At the same time, this does not lead him to believe that he should not make some sort of effort to find out; on the contrary, unless he does, he will not be able to draw up a defense, and he is an advocate whose function it is to defend accused persons. In the same fashion, even the free-lance advocates for whom Dr. Huld has contempt manage to devote energy to the pursuit of their calling. Upon the suspicion that the lowest grades in the Court contain corrupt and venal elements, these petty advocates try to "push their way in, by bribing and listening to gossip," and they are not above stealing documents if the opportunity should come their way.

But K., who has decided to ask his questions himself, lacks not only the energy to do so consistently, but suffers a weakness of such an order that he finds it difficult to concentrate upon his work as assessor. He cannot pay attention to the proposition which the manufacturer brings to him, nor summon enough strength even to interview the clients who are waiting for him outside his office. In fact, he cannot even take steps to counteract what he knows to be the strong likelihood that the Deputy Manager will take advantage of him and poison whatever good will the Manager himself may have towards him. He can neither function effectively as assessor nor can he contemplate the prospect of undertaking his own defense without incapacitating weariness: "What days were lying in wait for him? Would he ever find the right path through all

---

contrary, to suggest this would suggest that the doctors' testimony was faulty, which it could not be because there was no reason why they should not have told the complete truth. As a matter of fact, it was only by chance that the records were made available at all, and this was due entirely to the willingness of the Kennedy family, into whose hands they had somehow fallen, to deposit them, although not without some restrictions upon their use. The records were not public; "they could certainly, if the Court considered it necessary, become public, but the Law did not prescribe that they must be made public."

these difficulties? . . . Would he be able to survive?" He
recognizes that his powers are being sapped. At the same time
he has no doubt that if he were to devote himself energetically
and full-time to his defense, he would be acquitted. It would
be a policy which "would eventually bring about his absolute
and definite acquittal," but he feels so great a stupor that it
seems to him to be quite out of the question. His function of
assessor has been removed from him effectively by, and in
terms of, the act of arrest, so that he can no longer do what
he must do if it is to be performed. In this sense he continues
to destroy himself, by neglecting his business, by refusing to
accept the responsibility of seeing the businessmen who cluster
around him, by rushing away from his post at the bank in
order to see Titorelli, by mislaying agreements. It is, in effect,
a program of suicide, the abstraction of the death wish. In the
same manner he destroys himself with respect to his relationships with the Court: he speaks rudely to a magistrate who
might help him, and thus alienates him; he dismisses the
advocate Huld; he rejects the help of Leni; he takes little
notice of the advice of Titorelli and does not accept Titorelli's
offer to draw up a petition in due and proper form; he takes
no warmth from his uncle's concern and argues like a sophist
with the priest/prison chaplain. His wish for death produces
an increasing tiredness which can only end in the cessation of
movement; the life force, or energy, which the others enjoy, is
not for him. But this death wish is not offered in the character
of K. as representative of death wishes, nor as an invitation
to explore the conditions under which they become dominant,
with the implication that they need not. K. is the condition of
the dying man. His fatigue is inherent in his condition, and
its progressive quality is in fact the act, or the process, of
dying. We must return for a moment to an earlier proposition
that when man and his function are inseparable, man's function is inseparable from man's life. The loss of the one must

bring about the loss of the other; the weakening of the one
cannot occur without the weakening of the other. The only
way in which the life can be preserved, if a function should
disappear, is to assume another, but functions may not be
assumed until and unless they are authorized, until and unless
letters patent are issued. They cannot be assumed by an act
of individual volition. K.'s need, therefore, as his function/life
of assessor progressively withers away, is to receive a patent
for another function, to be readmitted, as we have pointed
out before, into the world if he is either too tired to take the
necessary steps, or insists that the world has no right to exclude
him in the first place. Nor can he gain this admission by himself. Since he has no right to it, he cannot demand it, but
can only ask for it, and a petitioner is always dependent
upon others because the form and the nature of the act of
petitioning are critically important. His attitude towards the
necessity of petitioning is itself ambiguous, because his death
wish would be frustrated if he were able to draw up a successful one. Moreover, if we consider his *as* dying man, in other
words, *as* the abstract image of death wish and the *condition*
which such a wish implies, he *cannot* fail to be ambivalent towards the requirements of the need for petitioning. It is not
a choice, but an inherent necessity, that he approach this
obligation with reservations. He continues therefore to make a
successful petition impossible because he does not recognize
its necessity as such, and is willing to accord it only that
expedient necessity which after a time he comes to acknowledge as being another unjustifiable requirement of a Court
which he cannot accept. If the Court is life, and if K. is com-
mitting suicide, he cannot of course ever come to accept the
Court. None the less, K.'s state of dying is not, as K. thinks,
necessarily the result of malevolent action. It may well be only
the punishment for being alive, and no man is innocent of
living, nor, living, fails to die at the same time. He becomes

increasingly weary as his assessor/function withers, because life, or strength, derives entirely from function, and is indivisible with it: its fortunes wax or wane in direct proportion. K.'s arrest has made his weariness, and his death, inevitable. Since he cannot receive an authorization—because he does not admit that there is any authority with the right to issue it, because he thinks that he has a right to live, because instead of applying, he uses the outmoded and supernumerary tools of his dying function—he cannot survive. He stands in his own way as the condition of dying stands in the way of the condition of surviving. He must remain, then, for the duration of the novel, suspended not only in the temporal limbo which has been noted previously, but in another limbo, that between life and death. But since he is in that limbo because his function has been lost, as the function disappears progressively he will move at the same speed towards death and towards an end to his suspended state.

It is noteworthy in this regard that the arrest is not immediately followed by any action. The Inspector says to K. almost at once that even though he is under arrest, "that need not hinder you from going about your business. You won't be hampered in carrying out the ordinary course of your life." The "ordinary course" of K.'s life is, among other things, that of dying and of wishing for death. His functions cannot be removed from him immediately, by, for example, an incarceration, because this would be violent and sudden death rather than the *process* of death, both in itself and as a concomitant of the death wish. And the *process* of death is that of rejecting, misunderstanding, frustrating and turning one's back on life. The questions asked about the nature of life accomplish this frustration: they enquire about what life means rather than about what life is, and in ignoring what life is, it is not possible to live it. If one does not live it, one dies, so that death is the punishment both for living life and for not living it. K. is removed from who and from what he was, and cannot become anything or anybody else, first because this is the nature of his removal, second because he does not really want to. In the due course of time his weakness will be such that its ultimate point can be *marked* by the thrust of a knife, not, as it appears, *caused*.

18.

The Death of Joseph K.

The "executioners" of the closing chapter are not therefore executioners at all, but serve to offer the framework of suicide. They lead him inexorably, having "fastened on him in a fashion he had never before seen or experienced," to a small quarry on the outskirts of town which is either the appointed place, or one which was only chosen because they were "too exhausted to go farther." As K. and the two men move towards the quarry, they are bound inextricably to each other, and move in such an integral fashion that they form a unity "such as can be formed almost by lifeless elements alone." There is no real distinction between K. and the men. They are not so much the instrumentalities of his approaching death as his approaching death itself, to which he is wedded in the intimate bond of condition. The condition of dying which is K., becomes in this fashion one with the act of dying itself. K. thus participates in his own death, for nobody can fail to participate in his own death. Indeed the dying man is the principal, and the only, actor on the stage.

K.'s awareness of the fact that the process of dying must be acted out takes the form of a projection to the men who are accompanying him, whom he invests with the reciprocal image of himself as actor. But K. is an egoist to begin with, and besides there can be no better actor in the play of dying than the dying man himself, who must give the best, as well as the only, performance. The first image is thus that of "tenth-rate old actors they send for me," with the implication "My death/part is not tenth-rate at all, but first—." leading him to say directly to the men "What theatre are you playing at?" Once the quarry is reached, and it is to the quarry that K. has been journeying for time out of mind, over so many countless and weary hours of toil and the sweat of the soul, the men carefully set the stage for what can only be suicide, since K. has been destroying himself and wishing for death. They remove his coat, waistcoat and shirt, folding them carefully; they keep him warm by walking him up and down while an exact point is being sought; they prop him against a boulder and settle his head upon it, and when despite all their efforts K. is still not properly and suitably disposed, one of the men takes it upon himself to arrange K. specially.

This is ceremony and ritual which presuppose that there is an importance in the manner of death. Importance in the manner, however, invests the death with another significance, that of being the culmination of an inevitable process which is, by the ritual, confirmed and reaffirmed. It must not only be done, but it must be done in a special way which has been laid down and cannot be altered without utterly destroying the affirmatory character. The men show no signs of intelligence; on the contrary they seem unable to answer a question which is outside their competence and, when K. asks them the unexpected question "What theatre are you playing at?", they can respond only like dumb men "struggling to overcome an unnatural disability." Yet, they know to the letter how their function is to be performed and can discern, and be disturbed by, irregularities such as K.'s "contorted and unnatural-looking" posture. The "correct" posture is that of suicide, and suicide is the confirming act of the death wish. K.'s inability to assume, or even to be placed in, the correct posture, stems from his refusal to accept the consequences of what he is, a refusal to be the immediate agent of his own death. The scene is set for suicide, but it is only after the men have passed the knife back and forth in front of K. for a number of times that he realizes that he is to use it himself, thus accepting his freedom and his responsibility. But he is too weak. He does not have the "remnant of strength necessary for the deed," and he will not give up his insistence upon placing the responsibility elsewhere: on the Court, on him "who had not left him the remnant of strength," on the universe, on God, on the world which rejected him, on anything outside of himself. "He could not relieve the officials of all their tasks," and while he perceives that he is in the midst of an occasion, he cannot "completely rise" to it. He must at the end, as he has throughout the novel, thwart and rebel against the process. In other terms, the wish for death and the wish for life are coextensive, like love and hate, and contain their own inherent ambiguity. K. is ambiguous, in consequence, to the end.

Still K.'s refusal to kill himself is neither a sign of weakness nor a sign of strength, and the character of the refusing K., much as he would appear to like it to serve as a symbol for dignity and for not "dying like a dog," does not function within the structure of this final chapter as representative of either weakness or of strength. There is, in the first place, no man "K." behind the man in the position of suicide, a man "K." who can choose or reject on the basis of a value system. K. *cannot* kill himself, for reasons which have nothing to do with a "K." who does not exist, but which relate, rather, to the nature of suicide itself and the way in which, in consequence, it functions within a literary work. The act of suicide in literature implies that the character who kills himself has

The Death of Joseph K.

chosen to kill himself after unfavorably considering the alternative of continuing to live, and that he has made this choice because the experience which he has assimilated in the course of the text has been summed up by him as indicating that choice as the better. The act of suicide is therefore often the figure of redemption, the structure of the assuagement of the qualm. Since it has this quality of serving as the figure of redemption, it postulates values to be redeemed, as well as an agent who understands those values sufficiently to enable him to act as agent. The suicide must be capable of assimilating experience, and must therefore be disjunctive from his experience at least to the point where he can view it and evaluate it. Since suicide is in its own nature a deliberate act, it cannot be divested of this element of deliberation. Where there is no deliberation there is no longer suicide, but accident, or murder, or cessation of certain functions for internal reasons. But K. is precisely unable to assimilate experience because he is the experience itself. He cannot be disjunctive from it, and hence cannot be agent for redemption, reaffirmation, or confirmation. Not only is he coeval with his own experience, he is this because there are no experiences apart from those who engage in them, no actions which have other than subjective settings. This is the nature of the universe and hence the nature of K., and is not even a particular quality of K. which we are to appreciate as an example of something. K. can therefore not, in view of his structural functions in the context of the novel, commit suicide. It is an alternative which simply does not exist; if it did exist, it could not do so without depending upon that disjunction between man and function which is essential to suicide in literature, and it would therefore falsify the novel and literally turn it right side up by turning it upside down. The novel would be another novel, and the novel *The Trial*, this single literary creation, would be gone. In that sense, this choice is no more open to Kafka than it is to K., and we should not appraise him in the light of the choice which he appears to have made: it has its own internal inevitability.

When death is not suicide (and it is not suicide when the element of deliberation has been removed from it), it is accident, murder, or cessation from "natural causes." Towards accident we have that horror which comes from the reminder that we are not safe in a contingent world which we cannot hope to control; towards cessation from "natural causes" we have an awareness of the mortality of man; towards murder we have an abreaction to its brutality. Brutality does not inhere in any given action. The plunging of a knife into one's own throat is not brutal because it contains a meaning within its pattern, but the plunging of a knife into the throat of somebody else, when this has been made necessary by his refusal to do it himself, becomes murder, and thus becomes brutal. The framework of suicide—the stage setting for the ritual, the ritual itself—which have been carefully prepared by the "executioners," requires only one further element to be complete, K.'s willingness to use the knife on himself. When he refuses to do this (as refuse he must), his death will not be postponed, but it will change in character and become only a bloody and brutal murder. K. will "die like a dog" because the only way not to die like a dog is to do what he cannot do. It is the same pattern as we find in *In the Penal Colony*. The elaborate machine, designed to be the instrument of redemption within a ritualistic pattern, is converted by the victim's illiteracy into a horrible machine of torture. Words carved into the flesh of the back which you cannot read become only sources of pain which, if tied to the machine, you have to suffer dumbly. The scene in the quarry is converted by K.'s refusal into a scene of brutal killing. But this is not only necessary because the option is essentially closed to K. to kill himself, it is necessary because this is the only kind of

The Death of Joseph K.

death which can serve as paradigm for K.'s insistence that
what has happened to him is somebody's else responsibility.
It is not possible to die by one's own hand and attribute the
responsibility of one's death to somebody else; by the same
token, death as victim of another's hand contains the other's
responsibility. Since K. *is* the condition of refusing the freedom
which comes from accepting freedom, he *cannot* die in any
other manner. The structure and the conditions which it carries
are indivisible; they are not examples of ideological or aesthetic
choices.

At the very end there seems to be a gossamer hint, an almost
imperceptible stirring of an awareness on the part of K. that
he is caught up in an absurd situation. "They look," he thinks
when he sees the executioners, "like tenors," and certainly
no remark has ever been made which better sums up not only
absurdity but the awareness of absurdity. He has certainly
reached the end of his road, and as Camus expresses it:

A un certain point de son chemin, l'homme absurde est
sollicité. . . . On lui demande de sauter. Tout ce qu'il peut
répondre, c'est qu'il ne comprend pas bien, que cela n'est
pas évident. Il ne veut faire justement que ce qu'il
comprend bien . . . On voudrait lui faire reconnaître sa
culpabilité. Lui se sent innocent. A vrai dire, il ne sent
que cela, son innocence irréparable. C'est elle qui lui
permet tout. Ainsi ce qu'il exige de lui-même, c'est de
vivre *seulement* avec ce qu'il sait, de s'arranger de ce qui
est et ne rien faire intervenir qui ne soit certain. On lui
répond que rien ne l'est. Mais ceci du moins est une
certitude. C'est avec elle qu'il a affaire: il veut savoir s'il
est possible de vivre sans appel.[31]

K. does not want to "die like a dog," but dogs do not know
they are dogs, and hence do not object to dying like them;
they can die no other way. K. expresses in this thought his

[31] Albert Camus, *Le Mythe de Sisyphe*, Paris: Gallimard, 1942,
pp. 75–76.

sense of the absurdity, and of the inappropriateness of his being snuffed out, an inappropriateness which for the only time in the novel, and then even very tentatively and vaguely, he does not ascribe to his innocence but to his human condition. There seems to be the suggestion that human life should be more than something which can end when, and because, a knife is struck into the throat. The death is wrong, somehow, not because it is not deserved, for K. is beyond that point, but because it lacks what can only be called "dignity." But the human condition is that of the dog—human life ends as swiftly, as meaninglessly, as brutally, and as inappropriately as any life ends. It is only a stage in a process and has no dignity in itself. It is possible, however, that Joseph K., too late as the man before the door was too late, has a glimmer of the light streaming through the door just prior to the final thrust of the knife which ends his life, that the absence of any inherent dignity can be transcended by acting as if it existed, by creating it through the affirmative act of postulating it. K. could have said, in effect "I die like a dog because I am a dog, but I affirm that I am something more and will die as if I were."

K. has never, of course, transcended, and can never transcend, his condition, because he is his condition and nothing more. The glimmer, if glimmer there was, fades quickly, and the literary image K., the only K. who has ever existed, stays within his imagistic limitations and sees his ignominious execution as a "shame" which will outlive him. He trusts that in the future somebody will say of him:

> Il ne se fit jamais un acte si cruel
> Mais c'est un témoignage à la race future
> Qu'on ne t'auroit su vaincre en un juste duel.[32]

But there was never any duel.

[32] Malherbe, *Sur la Mort d'un Gentilhomme qui fut assassiné.*

BIBLIOGRAPHY

Anders, Günther. *Franz Kafka*. New York: Hillary House Publishers, Ltd., 1960.

———— "Kafka: Ritual Without Religion," *Commentary*, VIII (December,1948), 560–569.

Arendt, Hannah. "Franz Kafka: a Revaluation," *Partisan Review*, XI (Fall,1944), 412–422.

Blanchot, Maurice. "Kafka et l'exigence de l'oeuvre," *Critique*, No. 58 (March,1952), 195–221.

———— "La Lecture de Kafka," *L'Arche*, No. 11 (November, 1945), 107–116.

Bodkin, Maud. *Archetypal Patterns in Poetry*. New York: Norton, 1949.

Boutonnier, Juliette. "Les Idées dans les Livres," *Psyché*, No. 54 (April,1951), 233–238.

Brod, Max. *Franz Kafka: eine biographie*. Prague: Heinrich Mercy sohn, 1937.

Brophy, Brigid. *Flesh*. London: Secker and Warburg, 1962.

Buber, Martin. *Two Types of Faith*. London and New York: Macmillan Company, 1951.

Burgum, Edwin Berry. "Franz Kafka and the Bankruptcy of Faith," *Accent*, III (Spring,1942) 154–167.

Burnham, James. "Observations on Kafka," *Partisan Review*, XIV (February,1947), 186–195.

Camus, Albert. *Le Mythe de Sisyphe*. Paris: Gallimard, 1942.

Carrouges, Michel. *Kafka contre Kafka*. Paris: Plon, 1962.

Choisy, Maryse. "Peut-on psychoanalyser un artiste?" *Psyché*, No. 54 (April,1951), 194–205.

Colie, Rosalie L. *Paradoxia Epidemica*. Princeton: Princeton University Press, 1966.

Daniel-Rops. "A French Catholic Looks at Kafka," *Thought*, XXIII (1948), 401–404.

Bibliography

Dauvin, René. *"The Trial:* Its Meaning," in *Franz Kafka Today,* ed. Flores and Swander. 145–160.

Flores, Angel and Swander, Homer (eds.) *Franz Kafka Today.* Madison: The University of Wisconsin Press, 1958.

Flores, Angel (ed.) *The Kafka Problem.* Norfolk, Conn.: New Directions, 1946.

Fremantle, Anne. "Every Relationship Between Man and God but One," *Commonweal,* LX (April 30,1954), 98–99.

——— "Kafka's Diaries," *Commonweal,* L (June 10,1949), 227–228.

Fuchs, Rudolf. "Social Awareness," in *The Kafka Problem,* 247–250.

Goodman, Paul. *Kafka's Prayer.* New York: Vanguard, 1947.

Goth, Maja. *Franz Kafka et les lettres françaises.* Paris: Librairie José Corti, 1956.

Gray, Ronald. *Kafka's Castle.* Cambridge University Press, 1956.

——— (ed.). *Kafka. A Collection of Critical Essays.* Englewood Cliffs, N.J.: Prentice-Hall, Inc., 1962.

Grene, Marjorie. *Dreadful Freedom; A Critique of Existentialism.* Chicago: University of Chicago Press, 1948.

Groethuysen, Bernard. "Apropos of Kafka," trans. Muriel Kittel, *Quarterly Review of Literature,* II:3 (Spring,1945), 237–249.

Holmes, Oliver Wendell. *The Autocrat of the Breakfast-Table.* Boston and New York: Houghton Mifflin Co., 1892.

Houselander, Carryl. *Guilt.* New York: Sheed and Ward, 1951.

Jones, Ernest. *Hamlet and Oedipus.* London: Oxford University Press, H. Milford, 1951.

Kelly, John. "Franz Kafka's *Trial* and the Theology of Crisis," *Southern Review,* V (Spring,1940), 748–766.

Kenner, Hugh. *Flaubert, Joyce and Beckett. The Stoic Comedians.* London: W. H. Allen, 1964.

Magny, Claude-Edmonde. "The Objective Depiction of Absurdity," trans. Angel Flores, *Quarterly Review of Literature,* II:3 (Spring,1945), 211–227.

Bibliography

Margeson, John. "Franz Kafka: A Critical Problem," *University of Toronto Quarterly*, XVIII (1948), 30–40.

Micha, René. "Le fantastique kafkaien sur le plan d'art," *L'Arche*, No. 16 (June,1946), 43–50.

Nadeau, Maurice. "Kafka et 'L'Assaut contre les Frontières,' " *Les Lettres Nouvelles*, No. 24 (February,1955), 260–267.

Nemeth, André. *Kafka ou le mystère juif*. Trans. Victor Hintz. Paris: J. Vigneau, 1947.

Nieder, Charles. *The Frozen Sea*. New York: Oxford University Press, 1948.

Rahv, Philip. "The Death of Ivan Ilych and Joseph K.," *Southern Review*, III (Summer,1939), 174–185.

Reiss, H. S. "Recent Kafka Criticism (1944–1955)—A Survey," in Boyd, J., Forster, L., and Magill, C. P., (eds.) *German Life and Letters*, Oxford: Basil Blackwell and Mott, 1943.

Robbe-Grillet, Alain. *For a New Novel*. Trans. Richard Howard. New York: Grove Press, 1965.

Robert, Marthe. *Kafka*. Paris: Gallimard, 1960.

Rochefort, Robert. *Kafka ou l'irréducible espoir*. Paris: R. Julliard, 1947.

———— "La culpabilité chez Kafka," *Psyché*, Nos. 18–19 (April–May,1948), 483–495.

Sarraute, Nathalie. "De Dostoievsky à Kafka," *Les Temps Modernes*, No. 25 (October,1947), 664–685.

Sartre, Jean-Paul. *The Flies*. Trans. Stuart Gilbert. New York: Vintage Books, n.d.

Spilka, Mark. *Dickens and Kafka*. Bloomington: Indiana University Press, 1963.

Stallman, Robert. "Kafka's Cage," *Accent*, VIII (1948), 117–125.

Tschumi, Raymond. *A Philosophy of Literature*. Philadelphia: Dufour Editions, 1962.

Tyler, Parker. "Kafka and the Surrealists," *Accent*, V (Autumn,1945), 23–27.

Unamuno y Jugo, Manuel de. *Tres Novelas y un Prólogo*. Madrid: Espasa-Calpe, S.A. (Colleción Contemporánea), n.d.

Bibliography

Uyttersprot, Hermann. "Zur Struktur von Kafkas Romanen," *Langues Vivantes*, XX (1954), 367–383.

——— "Zur Struktur von Kafkas 'Der Prozess.' Versuch einer Neuordnung," *Langues Vivantes*, XIX (1953), 333–376.

Vialatte, Alexandre. "L'histoire secrète du 'Procès,' " *Le Figaro Littéraire*, No. 78 (October 18,1947), 1–2.

Vivas, Eliseo. "Kafka's Distorted Mask," *Kenyon Review*, X (Winter,1948), 51–69.

Wahl, Jean. *Esquisse pour une histoire de l'existentialisme.* Paris: L'Arche, 1949.

Warren, Austin. "Franz Kafka," in *Rage for Order; Essays in Criticism.* Chicago: Chicago University Press, 1948.

Warshow, Robert. "Kafka's Failure," *Partisan Review*, XVI (April,1949), 4.

Webster, Peter Dow. "Arrested Individualism and the Problem of Joseph K. and Hamlet," *American Imago*, V (November, 1948), 4–23.

Will, Frederic. *Literature Inside Out.* Cleveland: The Press of Western Reserve University, 1966.

Wilson, Edmund. "A Dissenting Opinion on Kafka," *The New Yorker*, XXIII (July 26,1948), 58–64.